# A Mother's World

# A Mother's World

Edited by
Patricia Dreier

A READER'S DIGEST/C.R. GIBSON BOOK
Published by The C.R. Gibson Company, Norwalk, Connecticut 06856

The acknowledgments that appear on pages 94 and 95 are hereby made
a part of this copyright page.

A Reader's Digest/C.R. Gibson book published by arrangement
with The Reader's Digest Association, Inc., Pleasantville, N.Y.,
10570.

Printed in the United States of America.

ISBN: 0-8378-1805-2

# CONTENTS

# What Is A Mother?

*Who is a Mother? She knows what is important. That is why God asked them to be a mother.*

*Lizann*

*A mother is the only one if she sings your favorite song it stop thundering*

*Louise*

*It is lucky that we have a mother because if we did not have a mother everything would be in a big big mess.*

*Fred T.*

*A Mother is a person too.*

*David*

# BEGINNING TOGETHER, GROWING TOGETHER

# Diary Of A New Mother

*Mothers of all ages can share with one new mother the thrilling — and hectic — first six months of her baby's life.*

In one moment of undrugged physical release, our baby is thrust into the world, uniting us, husband and wife, in the communion of birth. We join hands as we watch his tiny face crumple in protest. My own body, so recently reaching into unknown reserves of energy, relaxes beneath a reviving flood of undiluted emotion. I share with women throughout the centuries the joy of bearing a child.

The baby, a startling fragile-looking creature, is handed to me for a moment and then to his father. I refuse to acknowledge my own awkwardness. Will I not somehow be endowed with the accumulated wisdom of mothers before me?

I am wheeled from the delivery room and permitted to watch my son's first bathing. Feeling entirely satisfied to let the nurse handle him, I dismiss as fantasy the notion that the process of giving birth mystically transforms a woman into a mother. And later, in my hospital room, I bask in the lingering glow of achievement, content to rest. Not until a few hours later does an instinctive hunger to cuddle my child and nourish him rise within me.

The nurse helps me prepare for this first nursing. Then she hands me a nest of soft wrappings that holds a tiny red face, mouth stretched wide. Instinct bobs his head back in a body-quivering search for the warm nipple. He is so trusting and I am so clumsy. And already he's asleep, his mouth open against my breast. Now motherhood is creeping over my old self like a long-awaited tomorrow that finally is today. I have lived it all again and again in my mind, but without the intoxication.

Even while he's asleep, his lips are remembering milk. His chin trembles unexpectedly; his body jerks without waking; his muscles respond to unwilled urges. I could spend half of each day just watching him.

Already, in his third day of life, the sound of my voice seems to have meaning for him. Milk will soothe him back into the sleep he never fully woke from. This newly discovered pleasure causes him to call out with impatience. To me his cry sounds rich and strong.

It seems so simple to put your baby on your shoulder and wait for a burp, but little knees used to being curled up to the chin leave you with a round baby ball that rolls down into your lap.

Carefully choosing from the travel case the exact baby clothes to suit the weather, I am aware that my husband and I are acting worse than newlyweds. We have that almost embarrassing pride gleaming in our eyes and the awkward meticulousness of our own just-assumed roles. The nurse removes our son's hospital garments and wraps his strangely long and straggly body in the over-sized going-home outfit that once looked so unbelievably small. Understanding nurses call good-by, and the elevator takes us down, a family now.

Out in the parking lot my husband dashes around in the fall drizzle, solicitously opening car doors, undoubtedly trying to stay in motion lest the nurse decide to hand him the baby. It's a little scary taking this helpless creature and driving off with him. What if he starts crying and I can't figure out how to stop him? I can't explain things to him — that he can trust me to feed him, change him, burp him or just hold him. And babies cry so loud. He won't understand that he doesn't have to let *everyone* know he's unhappy. Just me.

Our son is one week old. There he lies, flushed from yelling, his bowlegs attached below his abdomen where his hips will be, his softly curved arms attached below his ears where his shoulders will be.

11

He dominates my life. My days are a whirl of diapers and false-alarm hunger cries to be eased with a pacifier. My nights are a daze of half-heard wails answered with half-remembered feedings and a midnight rendezvous with the diaper pail. My former routines no longer serve me. I must concentrate on every movement and every minute until the mechanics are a part of me and motherhood allows me to resume my role as wife, sharing with my husband the wonder of being a parent.

We reflect upon our new status and decide there's nothing unusual about a new father's feeling terribly masculine and also terribly uninvolved in the three-ring circus his home has become.

Our son looks like a relic from a miniature monastery, with his long gown and smooth scalp. He fits the part of a tiny old holy man toothlessly wise. The only bits of world that penetrate into his hazy awareness are sudden bursts of light let in at random by his eyes. At times his whole being seems concentrated unblinkingly on a beam of light. Perhaps he's struggling with an idea too complex to absorb.

To have my baby take nourishment from my body, to see his eyes drift shut, to hear his purring contentment, is painfully exquisite. How many mothers spend their children's lives trying to satisfy their own urge to give and protect and be needed? *Now* is the time to give myself over to the cuddling and crooning, so that as his need diminishes I can loose my hold without regret.

Now at three months, I am suddenly faced with a crisis. As he sucks on his pacifier his grabbing fingers accidentally pull it out, leaving his mouth naked. Instinctively he plugs up the space between his lips with the built-in pacifier — his little mouth closes around his thumb. I watch apprehensively like a parent seeing her son sampling his first cigarette, envisioning him hooked on the habit but fearing to interfere. Fending off the warnings left by psychologists in my memory, I finally force myself to let my natural reactions guide me.

These newly acquired responsibilities are awesome. My gaze, voice, touch, have the power to bring about rewarding smiles, happy sounds and hearty eating, or they can encourage tears and fussy meals and frustrated thumb-sucking. I see motherhood ahead of me like an overgrown path that disappears into a dark woods. On one side is the fear of forcing a child into a mold not his own; on the other, the danger of leaving him to be molded by indifferent circumstances. Who am I to decide which behavior shall bring rewards and which reproof?

I am his mother.

Our son is four months old. The center of his world, the source of all pleasure and all unhappiness, is oral sensation. If he could fit the whole world into his mouth, he would understand all there is to know. He tries frantically to stretch his lips to admit both fists into the inner sanctum, the better to comprehend their purpose. His sausage feet loom before his eyes — within grabbing distance, but inaccessible to his waiting mouth.

And when he finally makes it over from his back to his belly, my husband and I realize that our own muscles have tensed, urging him on.

Secure within his hazy aura of mother love, he reaches out to his father. His eyes reveal the moment when indifference to this other familiar figure changes to recognition.

The baby's concentration is intense as he studies our eating movements. He mimics our simplest gestures. But also he has his own style of table manners: eagerly he dumps his peaches in my lap, slurps from his cup before plunking it to the floor, smears a handful of beets onto his high-chair tray, gleefully sneezes cereal in my face.

The half-year mark approaches, and the novelty of my breast as the milk machine is gone. His lips lose their hold on the nipple in the fascination of discovering a button or stroking my sweater's softness. I am prepared to surrender the lifeline of milk, knowing that his needs and mine must be one.

I watch our son perform award-winning roles, unconcerned about audience acclaim. He is a turtle accidentally stranded on a rock, frantically projecting head and limbs high in the air, but unable to budge; a victorious boxer, clasping hands overhead in triumph. He is The Thinker, scratching pensively behind his ear; a Lilliputian superman with his bib flung over the shoulders.

I nurse him for the last time, savoring the ritual about-to-be-memory. My thoughts go back to when he emerged from the womb, clothed only in innocence, skilled only in searching. Soon he will unlock the mysteries of self-propulsion. One dare not think of the terrible void that will be left by the absence of this tiny, incredibly lovable being.

But motherhood sweeps away all thoughts of the impermanence of the human body in a wild exhilaration of love and dreams, and the bearable ache of letting go little by little, day by day. As my child struggles to sit, to search out the sounds and feel of the world, I sense that my role these six months has been beneath him, supporting. From now on my role will be from above, lifting.

Motherhood feels comfortable.

Judith Geissler

AUTHOR'S NOTE: *Although the message of motherhood is timeless, I have a special hope in these days of combining careers with babies that parenthood will continue to be lifted up as a sacred trust between parents and the Creator of life.*

*The three most beautiful sights: a potato garden in bloom,
a woman after the birth of her child.*

*Irish proverb*

## Mothers' Arms

When my second daughter was born, my mother came to
help me with the new baby and my 14-month-old toddler.
On one occasion, when both girls were fussing and wet, my
husband remarked, "At times like this, I think God should
have made mothers with four arms."

"He did," replied my mother with a smile. "But two of
them are on the fathers."

*Susan D. Skoor*

## Time Out For "Sesame Street"

My daughter gave up a successful business career to become a full-time mother to her three small children. Recently, she entertained her husband's boss and his wife. This impeccably groomed matron launched into a long discourse about the many organizations in which she was involved, and about her various creative activities. Finally, she asked my daughter the inevitable question: "And what do you do in your spare time, my dear?"

Serenely, my daughter replied, "I watch 'Sesame Street.'"

*D. L. G.*

## "This Little Piggy"

When my wife quit work to take care of our new baby daughter, countless hours of peekaboo and other games slowly took their toll.

One evening, she smacked her bare toes on the corner of a dresser and, grabbing her foot, sank to the floor. I rushed to her side and asked where it hurt. She looked up at me through tear-filled eyes and managed to moan. "It's the piggy that ate roast beef."

*Gary Burnett*

# Four

Four is too big for his breeches,
Knows infinitely more than his mother,
Four is a matinee idol
To Two-and-a-Half, his brother.
Four is a lyric composer,
Raconteur extraordinaire,
Four gets away with murder,
Out of line, and into hair.
Where Four is, there dirt is also,
And nails and lengths of twine,
Four is Mr. Fix-it
And all of his tools are mine.
Four barges into everything
(Hearts, too) without a knock.
Four will be five on the twelfth of July.
And I wish I could stop the clock.

*Elise Gibbs*

# Let The Screen Door Slam

*Ah, those warm, delicious, nothing-to-do days of childhood summer!*

This old house has never been treated to the newfangled metal screen doors that sigh discreetly as they close. Ours are wooden and hooked to protesting springs. A hundred times a day they squeal open and clatter shut. That many times a day I open my mouth to say, "Don't let the door slam." Ninety-nine times I say nothing. It's a summer sound from my own childhood. I like to hear it.

When the screen door slams, I smell phlox in a garden that no longer exists. I see daisies in a field, waiting to be braided into chains. I feel the hot boards of a sunbaked porch under my bare feet, sense the prickle of a peeling sunburn on my back.

What summer used to be, so it still is for my children. If bathing suits no longer itch, poison ivy does, and it's as delicious as ever to scratch. The ice-cream man may not be the adventure he was before freezers, but surely cool vanilla tastes no less wonderful melting on the tongue. This generation of phlox is as fragrant as the old; murder with a fly-swatter continues to be satisfying; and I suppose (though I haven't tried it lately) it still hurts cruelly to take a brave, belly-whopping smack into icy water.

I know, without his telling me, what it is like for my smallest son to wake up before the rest of us. He dresses in yesterday's dungarees and goes out unwashed and unbreakfasted to exult in the importance of being early and alone. He climbs into a tree, hangs there by his knees, and tests the effects of upside-down. Relaxed as a sloth, he says an inverted good-morning to the milkman.

I had such mornings once, and so did you.

My son descends to earth and his breakfast: a peach and a muffin eaten beneath the tree. If he lies on his stomach, he can watch ants laboring through a grassy forest with his crumbs. If he rolls to his back, he can look infinitely up past leaves and nests, discovering that space is great and the world is small — but marvelous. There's a lot for a child to think about in summer.

Or not. I don't imagine that when my three go off on their bikes they consciously count their blessings. They pedal through a meadow, hay-scented and shrill with insects, toward where the river has made a swimming hole and neighbors have built a jumping-off place. Trees hang over, the sun filters through, and the rare adults who intrude are only parents, too full of summer languor to make rules. It's a little kingdom of children, fish and waterbugs.

Nine waterlogged, ravening children may come for lunch, or none. I rarely know, or care much, which it will be. For days at a time, my children live abroad, returning here only when starving or lacking a bed. Then there are days when I can hardly move for the bodies strewn about, and every loaf of bread disappears as quickly as a burst balloon.

They live in cycles: eating out, playing out, sleeping out, then giving over whole days and nights to Monopoly in the living room. Piles of sweaty money are passionately guarded. Houses and hotels go up and into bankruptcy. Friendships fail. At the very height of financial fever, they abandon all to run before a hose in bathing suits.

Badminton, played until the last birdie is lost in the hedge. Croquet, until the cheating is too flagrant for forgiveness. Checkers. Old Maid. Fist fights. Grass tasted and examined. Prickers and blisters admired. The sun soaking in. Philosophy, nonsense, and talk of movies.

Sooner or later the pack disperses. One child, provendered with peanut-butter sandwiches, moves into his rediscovered tree house. The second bakes a cake and sits on the back steps licking frosting from the beaters. The third retreats to the dimness of his room and takes up the life of a hermit, doing push-ups, reading old *National Geographics,* or just watching newborn kittens climb the mountain of his blankets.

In a thousand ways they divert themselves, as we have done, you and I. We know *every* summer pastime, from rocking on a porch and slapping at mosquitoes, to digging a hole so deep the dirt at the bottom is cool.

One day in August, my children will say there is nothing to do. They'll sit listlessly on rope swings, prodding themselves into merest motion with one toe, or sprawl on the glider making the springs creak, creak, creak like a complaint. There's nothing to eat, they'll say, standing glumly before a refrigerator spilling food. If we only had a horse, a boat, a swimming pool, they'll say. They'll leave the record player to scratch out the same tune 20 times, mechanically insisting on monotony.

Nothing to do, they'll say. All unaware, they are rushing toward a time when they'll look back on this summer with wistful remembering — when they are grown, like you and me, wishing for long days of such nothings to do.

Joan Mills

# When Fall Came In On Roller Skates

"How do you know when fall gets here?" a five-year-old asked her mother and me one droopy September Sunday afternoon when the temperature was 92 degrees.

"Fall is when the leaves are red and the air is nippy and you get to wear your new wool clothes," said her mother. "In fact, fall starts officially next week."

The child, taking in the used-green leaves and the heat miasma uncoiling from the patio, clearly regarded this as another piece of adult propaganda, and rewarded us with the level stare children reserve for adult excesses. Wool, bright foliage and tart mornings were light-years away from her back yard.

It was probably a rhetorical question. Children know when autumn comes, almost to the hour. Some small signal forever lost to adults trips a delicate interior alarm clock. It isn't leaves going bright, or cool mornings. Those come later. Fall comes when you stop doing the summer things and start doing the fall ones.

When I was small, fall came in on roller skates. Somewhere in the last burning days of August, a morning came when we met as usual and the skates were there, jangling in bicycle baskets. Skate keys sprouted amulet-like around reedy necks, on shoelaces or grimy twine. There had been no previous agreement to put away the rubber-tire slingshots and the gut-spilling softballs. The alarm clock had simply, for each of us, gone off sometime in the dreamless night.

For the rest of fall, up until the lowering winter met us on the way home from school and robbed us of the light, skating was the autumn thing that we did. We went in swooping flights down sidewalks and streets, always with our parents' "Be careful!" thrumming in our ears, drunk on our own momentum, giddy on wind and wheels. The very small ones of us, restricted to front walks, windmilled on treacherous feet and looked with awe and hate at the flying phalanxes of big kids streaming by, trailing immortality like a comet's bright tail.

We came to know every street, every sidewalk, by the burring skirr our skates made on them; they spoke to us in a hundred voices, through the soles of our feet. Each of us, every fall, ruined a pair of shoes with too-tight skate clamps. Knees were scabbed until Christmas.

School started somewhere in the yellowing days, and we went back to the rows of scarred desks. We were strange to each other for a little while, even though we'd been together for a whole summer. But soon we were the spawn of chalk and cloakrooms again, creatures of a thousand rituals, and the wild summer children were gone. Tans went mustardy and flaked. Big colts' feet, bare and winged like Hermes' all summer, were now earthbound as Clydesdales' in clunking new saddle oxfords. Rasping sweaters began to feel good in the mornings as we jostled to school, flanked by an honor guard of trotting dogs.

Summer was a time of good things to eat, of course, but it is the taste of autumn that I remember. Wild, smoky, bitter-sweet things ripened in the bronze afternoons, and the glazed mornings bit them to exotic sharpness. Preposterous yellow persimmons grew on a tree in the schoolyard, and if you got a good one, the taste was incredible, like a topaz melting on your tongue. Flinty little apples lay on the ground under the old trees in the ruined orchard, each one worth one bite of pure, winy nectar before you noticed half a worm. Sweet potatoes, newly dug from their sand hills and roasted in my grandmother's black coal stove, were honey and smoke, too rich to finish.

As the fall wore on, mornings were born silver, and bleeding sunsets arrived earlier, and rumbling furnaces came alive in basements. The county fair wheeled by in a Technicolor blur of sawdust and cotton candy, and forbidden midway shows where, the big kids said, ladies took their clothes off. Halloween smelled of the wet, burnt insides of pumpkins. I remember one magic night in October when I was plucked up out of sleep, wrapped in a quilt, and taken outside in our back yard to watch a meteor shower. Warm on my father's shoulder, but with everything strange and too big and not like our back yard at all, I watched as the sky above me arced and bloomed. It was, I thought, something God arranged for me because he knew my father.

Soon ice crystals bristled in red clay, waiting to be scrunched under the loathsome galoshes. Saturdays and Sundays, which had been vast blue bowls to whoop and tumble in, turned gray and howled. We did smeary things with scissors and paste, and drove our parents wild, whining plaintively about the eternities of our heavy days.

We listened, with much the same look as my young friend in the patio, to their patient recounting of the fun we'd have next spring. But that was next year. And between us and spring, as the fall came down like a black window shade, lay the long, whirling winter.

Anne Rivers Siddons

## *End Of Summer*

*Summer is losing some of its wattage;*
*The pipes are oozing down at the cottage.*
*Golf greens are browning; baseball is pallid;*
*Nobody's downing potato salad.*
*Kids are despairing; but all of the while,*
*Mothers are wearing the ghost of a smile.*

*Betty Billipp*

23

# "Okay, Mom, If I Take The Car?"

*A story about growing up.*

There was nothing in my mind that afternoon except counting out the right number of candles for a cake. (Sixteen of them. My, it doesn't seem possible.) The birthday boy came strolling in from school then and, instead of sticking his fingers in the icing, said, "Come on, Mom, take me to get my temps?"

"What are temps?"

"My temporary learner's permit," he explained with great patience.

Well, how would I know? True, he had told me he was signed up for driver's education at school, but he often announces things like the West Coast is washing away at the rate of two feet a year, so I don't usually attach much urgency to his information.

Besides, if he's old enough to drive, how come the training wheels off his bike are still falling out of the garage cupboard? Answer me that!

My mumbled objections are ignored, and away we go to get the permit.

Even in driver-education courses, the student gets only an hour a week behind the wheel. Therefore, after professional instruction has begun, the student should practice on his own. Naturally, one of the parents must supervise and, naturally, "one of the parents" means Mother. So I soon find myself on the passenger side with an objective viewpoint and a detached calmness that they say often comes with pure terror.

My son has explained to me that his eyes are so much keener than mine, his reflexes are so much snappier, and his training is so superior that I gather I will be more an appreciative audience than a helpful mentor and will probably pick up a few pointers from him. And so, when another car comes toward us between two parked cars on a narrow street and his eyes go wide and his foot trembles on the brake and he stammers, "Wha-wh-what'll I do?" I must admit it feels kind of good.

"You're the driver; you decide," I hear my voice saying. He bites his lip, pulls over, lets the other car through and goes on. I find I have not held my breath long enough to faint, but it was close.

It is very important not to criticize a student while he is driving. If he makes some mistake, wait until he stops, get your heart and throat disentangled and suggest that, as stop signs can be seen a block away, he needn't wait until the last 30 feet before slamming on the brake.

Eventually, he completes the course, passes his test and gets his license. You'd think he'd be satisfied. But, no! Now he wants to drive the car!

Right away we made a few rules. He could drive on Sunday afternoons between two and four, provided visibility was clear for two miles, he didn't go over 30 and made no left turns.

But deep in my mind a small idea began to grow. Why was I continually dashing out of the house, feet in slippers, hair in rollers on some last-minute errand, when the State of Ohio (which certainly ought to know) had declared I had a perfectly fit substitute? Especially one whose idea of heaven was to drive a car.

In a week we were sending him out at five minutes to midnight for a loaf of bread and halfway across the state to take his sister to Grandma's. But the other side of that is, he should have the car when he needs it.

The places he suddenly *needed* to go to were hard to believe. It invariably took six trips downtown to buy one record.

If he went out for potato chips, I think he bought one chip at a time. Every night his homework took him to the library, although up to now homework had not played a large part in his life.

He developed a smooth operation of coming in the back door, hooking the keys off the refrigerator and calling out, "Okay if I take the car? I gotta go loofosoleafonmbioclss."

"What did you say?" I holler. By that time he is turning the corner.

There's no getting around it; one boy plus four wheels equals independence. If he could drive to the barber and the shopping center, he could also choose his own hairstyle and pick out his clothes.

After a while, his hair didn't seem so long and, if we didn't learn to love lavender tie-died jeans, we learned not to flinch. On vacations, he took his turn driving the freeways with a skill and confidence we had to admire. It occurred to us he might also be able to handle his school schedule without us hanging over his neck, wringing our hands.

Instead of begging with a note of hysteria, "What are you going to *do* with your life?" we asked with genuine interest, "What are you going to do with your life?" Turned out he had some sensible plans.

All these things came about slowly; no big deal—just a more relaxed atmosphere. He started hanging around the kitchen so much that I showed him a few tricks about cooking. In turn, he taught me guitar chords.

I didn't realize how much had changed until one day our youngest stumbled in screaming, with blood dripping down his face. Blotting it up, I nearly panicked at the jagged cut next to his eye, and would have, too, except for the strong hand on my arm and the calm voice saying, "It doesn't seem deep near his eye; let's get him to the hospital."

At that moment, all I could remember about hospitals was that they placed great value on cleanliness and Johnny was a grubby, four-year-old mess.

"We can't take him anyplace looking like this," I said in confusion.

"Don't claim him. Pretend you found him someplace," my teen-ager advised. "Tune it down, John."

Johnny tuned down to a whimper, and we drove off to the emergency room for ten stitches.

On my way home, with Johnny on my lap, I looked in wonder at my son beside me.

"How come," I asked, "after years of driving me batty, you've turned into a wonderful human being?"

"I don't know, Mom," he answered, without taking his eyes off the road, "but it's a funny thing—I've been wondering the same thing about you."

Catherine Lavarnway

*Courage is bringing a child into the world, feeding him and clothing him, caring for him and worrying about him, disciplining him and educating him, preparing him to the best of your ability for the life he is going to lead. And then letting him live it.*

D. L. Stewart

## The Virtue Of Casualness

*God knows that a mother needs fortitude and courage and tolerance and flexibility and patience and firmness and nearly every other brave aspect of the human soul. But because I happen to be a parent of almost fiercely maternal nature, I praise casualness. It seems to me the rarest of virtues. It is useful enough when children are small. It is important to the point of necessity when they are adolescents. The young on their way to maturity long for privacy, physical and spiritual. They resent being too well understood, and they abhor having their emotions dragged into the light. Mothers who can forbear to pry and question, who have the self-possession to let children weather their own storms, who, above all, respect confidences but do not demand them, will find those same confidences being given without demand. And their children will be stronger persons. Or so one hopes.*

*Phyllis McGinley*

# TEACHING
# AND
# LEARNING

# The Lesson Of
# The Fire Flowers

They say never go back. But it was a day for going back. Flocks of clouds grazed across the sky. Speckled quail rustled in the underbrush. And the song of the locust vibrated through hickory hills and oak valleys. Everyone knows such a day — a day for returning to childhood to see if that bygone life was what you'd thought!

Far away from the university where my husband teaches and the suburbs where we live, I sought a place where summer dwells in depth. Beyond dusty roads lined with goldenrod, I found the turnoff to the valley of my childhood. I watched for a figure picking berries — slim bronze legs striding against white starched skirts. But my mother had not passed this way for years. And the slimness and the stride were long past, too.

I did not even think of the roses then, nor of the strange feeling of respect that they always stir within me. But I did think of Mr. Riley, the man who grew that special species of rose, as I passed the hillside farm once his. And I hurried on, for the valley called to someone deep within me — a girl of ten with eyes too big for her face and Buster-Brown hair.

It was she, more than I, who topped the crest to see a chimney jutting from the trees, then gasped at the naked foundation of the house. Heedless of deed holder, a wilderness of blackjack oak possessed the land — much as it had when we first camped in a lean-to while my father built the house.

Father had been a product of the country, without a ready market in the city. But that realization had come late to him and the chance to return to the farm even later. By the April we moved from the city slums, my father was gaunt and gray. Pursued by a chronic lung condition, he fled to nature and the dream of a valley farm.

But my mother had seen his dreams dissolve before. Some 20 years younger than Father, her youth and vigor always contrasted to his age and frailty. With compassionate eyes, she watched him working and saw the rest times grow more numerous. She saw him go pale and lean against the young oaks.

When my father finally went away to the sanatorium, she set about learning the land. White starched kerchief mooring her long black hair, she plowed the meadow into a garden and set up brooder house and barn. I helped her to milk the cows and feed the chickens, to hoe and to plant, while my 14-year-old sister, Jo, kept house and cooked.

One summer's twilight, two figures topped the hill. "It must be Mr. Riley and his daughter!" Jo called excitedly. We were all anxious to meet our only close neighbor, Mr. Riley, who had been away all winter working in Fort Smith. Soft lamp glow highlighted red hair, gray eyes and ruddy complexion. I was surprised to see that the same rawboned features made the father handsome and the daughter — 16-year-old Bell — homely. But it was the bouquet Mr. Riley handed Mother that claimed my curiosity. "What kind of flower is that?" I asked, staring at the strange, beautiful blossoms.

"It's a rose that I crossbred." Mr. Riley's voice was deep and pleasant. "I call this species Fire Flowers."

The name appropriately described fragile petals of velvet fire that curled about yellow centers. As Mother carefully arranged the bouquet, Mr. Riley looked at her smiling face, her dark eyes, her tiny gold earrings, and saw a kinship to the roses.

By the time we had eaten a loaf cake fresh from the oven with cold buttermilk, Mother had learned how to get two crops per year from the meadow. She had also learned something that stirred her sympathy. Mr. Riley's wife had died when Bell was three, and he knew that she needed a mother now, more than ever. It seemed that Bell could sit a tractor and plow like a man, but as a woman she was clumsy, shy, unhandy at cooking and sewing. Mother, who was more than sympathetic, offered to help the girl become more feminine. She suggested that Bell join the Sunday-school classes which she conducted for us in our kitchen.

The formal classes were scarcely a disguise for the home-making lessons that Mother devised. Every Sunday Bell would come bouncing over the hill in some ancient get-up from her mother's trunk. And she'd leave with a more graceful gait, her dress subtly transformed by basting here and tucking there.

After Sunday school, Mother would put on a chicken to fry and show Bell how to cook. When Mr. Riley arrived, Mother would announce as all of us beamed, "Bell fried the chicken." If Mr. Riley was happy at his daughter's progress, he was mesmerized by her teacher.

I, too, was mesmerized by my mother's abilities, particularly her fearlessness. She fended off foxes and hawks with nothing more than a garden hoe, and chopped to death poisonous copperheads drawn too near the cistern. I thought her utterly fearless until that day in late August.

A dirty-yellow sky had threatened rain all day and a hollow stillness hung over the valley. Mother went to the field and gathered the last cucumbers and tomatoes. As she approached the house, she heard a frightening noise in a brush pile near the steps. Peering into the pile, she glimpsed a terrifying creature — a huge black monster with green head and giant green fangs.

Mother's hands shook as she came up the steps, dumped her apron and reached for her hoe. "Jo," she said, struggling to steady her voice, "you go get Mr. Riley. Jeanne, you stay in the house. I'm going out to stand guard at the brush pile until Mr. Riley gets here."

It seemed an eternity before Mr. Riley arrived, scooped mother to one side, and pointed his shotgun into the brush pile. Then, quite suddenly, he lowered the gun and leaned down to take a better look.

"Is that your monster?" he asked Mother gently, smiling and pointing into the brush. "Come here," he said, "and look closely at an ordinary black snake whose appetite is bigger than his mouth. That's a huge green frog, stuck half in and half out of his mouth. Those 'fangs' are the frog's legs."

That was when Mother finally broke. Tears rolled down her cheeks, and she slumped forward. But Mr. Riley moved quickly enough to catch her small collapsing figure. And right then I knew that things could never be the same again.

As thunder pierced the hollow stillness, I looked at Mother and suddenly knew her secret. She was desperately afraid — and had been all along — of the foxes, the hawks, the copperheads. But she had faced them anyway! No more would I be amazed at her fearlessness, but I would ever marvel at her enormous courage. I became aware of something else, too . . . of the tender way Mr. Riley was holding Mother, the way his eyes burned as he looked at her. In his strong arms, Mother soon stopped crying. She pulled gently free and regained her composure by making some lemonade. But Mr. Riley had lost his for good.

He could no longer sit still in the same room with Mother. No longer could he watch her in the lamplight without claiming her for his own. But he saw her as a woman who would carefully weigh desire and decency, and he knew which she would choose. So he stayed away.

Then, one afternoon, Mr. Riley "brought Bell to visit outside" with Jo and me, while he went into the house to talk to Mother. We three girls sat around the cistern, cool to our bare feet, but my mind was on the couple in the house. They were teetering on the brink of something, just like the pebbles I had stacked on the edge of the cistern wall. I pushed one pebble and they all fell into the water. I looked toward the house, frightened. I loved my mother and Mr. Riley both. But, if they fell in, something would be removed from my love — something! What was that something?

I sat wondering about it when Mr. Riley came to the door with Mother. He looked disappointed, as though he were arguing a point he'd already lost. "But in Fort Smith, who would know?" he was saying.

*"They* would!" Mother nodded toward us girls. "And *we* would! Oh, Riley! Don't *you* know if I were the kind of woman to divorce a man who down-and-out needs me, I wouldn't be the kind of woman you'd want to marry?"

He looked at her a long moment and saw the truth, for her sense of rightness was partly what he loved. "You're right," he rasped, as if the words burned his throat. Then he called Bell, said "Good-by" and walked up the hill toward home.

The next and last time I saw the Rileys, they had sold the farm and were moving to Fort Smith. Mr. Riley carried a large newspaper bundle in his arms. "I brought you the Fire Flower bush," he said simply. "Where should I plant it?"

"Right beside the step," Mother answered. I got the spade and watched him plant the large bush.

Now, with little left of my valley except the wilderness, I stared across the meadow to the foundation of the house. And there were those special roses! Not only growing from the step, but covering a whole section of the yard. I understood the feeling of respect that roses always stir within me. Respect was that something I had feared would be removed from my love for Mother and for Mr. Riley. Respect, a splendid legacy, now flourished in my heart as the Fire Flowers flourished in the valley.

Jeanne Hill

# The Day Mother Cried

Coming home from school that dark winter's day so long ago, I was filled with anticipation. I had a new issue of my favorite sports magazine tucked under my arm, and the house to myself. Dad was at work, my sister was away, and Mother wouldn't be home from her new job for an hour. I bounded up the steps, burst into the living room and flipped on a light.

I was shocked into stillness by what I saw. Mother, pulled into a tight ball with her face in her hands, sat at the far end of the couch. She was crying. I had never seen her cry.

I approached cautiously and touched her shoulder. "Mother?" I said. "What's happened?"

She took a long breath and managed a weak smile. "It's nothing, really. Nothing important. Just that I'm going to lose this new job. I can't type fast enough."

"But you've only been there three days," I said. "You'll catch on." I was repeating a line she had spoken to me a hundred times when I was having trouble learning or doing something important to me.

"No," she said sadly. "There's no time for that. I can't carry my end of the load. I'm making everyone in the office work twice as hard."

"They're just giving you too much work," I said, hoping to find injustice where she saw failure. She was too honest to accept that.

"I always said I could do anything I set my mind to," she said. "And I still think I can in most things. But I can't do this."

I felt helpless and out of place. At age 16 I still assumed Mother could do anything. Some years before, when we sold our ranch and moved to town, Mother had decided to

35

open a day nursery. She had had no training, but that didn't stand in her way. She sent away for correspondence courses in child care, did the lessons and in six months formally qualified herself for the task. It wasn't long before she had a full enrollment and a waiting list. Parents praised her, and the children proved by their reluctance to leave in the afternoon that she had won their affection. I accepted all this as a perfectly normal instance of Mother's ability.

But neither the nursery nor the motel my parents bought later had provided enough income to send my sister and me to college. I was a high-school sophomore when we sold the motel. In two years I would be ready for college. In three more my sister would want to go. Time was running out, and Mother was frantic for ways to save money. It was clear that Dad could do no more than he was doing already — farming 80 acres in addition to holding a full-time job.

Looking back, I sometimes wonder how much help I deserved. Like many kids of 16, I wanted my parents' time and attention, but it never occurred to me that they might have needs and problems of their own. In fact, I understood nothing of their lives because I looked only at my own.

A few months after we'd sold the motel, Mother arrived home with a used typewriter. It skipped between certain letters and the keyboard was soft. At dinner that night, I pronounced the machine a "piece of junk."

"That's all we can afford," Mother said. "It's good enough to learn on." And from that day on, as soon as the table was cleared and the dishes were done, Mother would disappear into her sewing room to practice. The slow tap, tap, tap went on some nights until midnight.

It was nearly Christmas when I heard her tell Dad one night that a good job was available at the radio station. "It would be such interesting work," she said. "But this typing isn't coming along very fast."

"If you want the job, go ask for it," Dad encouraged her.

I was not the least bit surprised, or impressed, when

Mother got the job. But she was ecstatic.

Monday, after her first day at work, I could see that the excitement was gone. Mother looked tired and drawn. I responded by ignoring her.

Tuesday, Dad made dinner and cleaned the kitchen. Mother stayed in her sewing room, practicing. "Is Mother all right?" I asked Dad.

"She's having a little trouble with her typing," he said. "She needs to practice. I think she'd appreciate it if we all helped out a bit more."

"I already do a lot," I said, immediately on guard.

"I know you do," Dad said evenly. "And you may have to do more. You might just remember that she is working primarily so you can go to college."

I honestly didn't care. In a pique I called a friend and went out to get a soda. When I came home the house was dark, except for the band of light showing under Mother's door. It seemed to me that her typing had got even slower. I wished she would just forget the whole thing.

My shock and embarrassment at finding Mother in tears on Wednesday was a perfect index of how little I understood the pressures on her. Sitting beside her on the couch, I began very slowly to understand.

"I guess we all have to fail sometime," Mother said quietly. I could sense her pain and the tension of holding back the strong emotions that were interrupted by my arrival. Suddenly, something inside me turned. I reached out and put my arms around her.

She broke then. She put her face against my shoulder and sobbed. I held her close and didn't try to talk. I knew I was doing what I should, what I could, and that it was enough. In that moment, feeling Mother's back racked with emotion, I understood for the first time her vulnerability. She was still my mother, but she was something more: a person like me, capable of fear and hurt and failure. I could feel her pain as she must have felt mine on a thousand occasions when I had sought comfort in her arms.

Then it was over. Wiping away the tears, Mother stood and faced me. "Well, son, I may be a slow typist, but I'm not a parasite and I won't keep a job I can't do. I'm going to ask tomorrow if I can finish out the week. Then I'll resign."

And that's what she did. Her boss apologized to her, saying that he had underestimated his workload as badly as she had overestimated her typing ability. They parted with mutual respect, he offering a week's pay and she refusing it. A week later Mother took a job selling dry goods at half the salary the radio station had offered. "It's a job I can do," she said simply. But the evening practice sessions on the old green typewriter continued. I had a very different feeling now when I passed her door at night and heard her tapping away. I knew there was something more going on in there than a woman learning to type.

When I left for college two years later, Mother had an office job with better pay and more responsibility. I have to believe that in some strange way she learned as much from her moment of defeat as I did, because several years later, when I had finished school and proudly accepted a job as a newspaper reporter, she had already been a reporter with our hometown paper for six months.

Mother and I never spoke again about the afternoon when she broke down. But more than once, when I failed on a first attempt and was tempted by pride or frustration to scrap something I truly wanted, I would remember her selling dresses while she learned to type. In seeing her weakness I had not only learned to appreciate her strengths, I had discovered some of my own.

Not long ago, I helped Mother celebrate her 62nd birthday. I made dinner for my parents and cleaned up the kitchen afterward. Mother came in to visit while I worked, and I was reminded of the day years before when she had come home with that terrible old typewriter. "By the way," I said. "Whatever happened to that monster typewriter?"

"Oh, I still have it," she said. "It's a memento, you know . . . of the day you realized your mother was human. Things are a lot easier when people know you're human."

I had never guessed that she saw what happened to me that day. I laughed at myself. "Someday," I said, "I wish you would give me that machine."

"I will," she said, "but on one condition."

"What's that?"

"That you never have it fixed. It is nearly impossible to type on that machine and that's the way it served this family best."

I smiled at the thought. "And another thing," she said. "Never put off hugging someone when you feel like it. You may miss the chance forever."

I put my arms around her and hugged her and felt a deep gratitude for that moment, for all the moments of joy she had given me over the years. "Happy birthday!" I said.

The old green typewriter sits in my office now, unrepaired. It *is* a memento, but what it recalls for me is not quite what it recalled for Mother. When I'm having trouble with a story and think about giving up, or when I start to feel sorry for myself and think things should be easier for me, I roll a piece of paper into that cranky old machine and type, wor d by painful wor d, just the way Mother did. What I remember then is not her failure, but her courage, the courage to go ahead.

It's the best memento anyone ever gave me.

Gerald Moore

# A Gift Of Freedom

*My daughter is not yet three years old. Without her, I would not have seen, lodged in a crack in a Brooklyn pavement, a grain of soot. "What is it?" she asks, crouching down. "Pick it up for me," she demands. "It's pretty." It is the first time I have studied a grain of soot; it is perfectly round, glossy as polished obsidian, beautiful.*

*My children restore to me a part of the world which usually retreats, just out of reach, in the face of my scurrying. Without my child, I would have missed not only the grain of soot but an opportunity for complete absorption in something other than myself — which is a kind of freedom.*

Phyllis La Farge

# Happiness Is . . .

*I was feeling guilty and inadequate because, for the third morning in a row, my son had to wait while I ironed a shirt for him to wear to school. But a visit to Mike's third-grade classroom that night changed my perspective and restored my self-esteem. On a bulletin board, with other papers listing "Three Things That Make Me Happy," Mike had written: "Happiness is putting on a shirt that's still warm from being ironed."*

Mary E. Atchley

# It's Not Whether
# You Win Or Lose . . .

*For one small boy, it's definitely how you play the game.*

When my son, Johnny, was in the third grade, he entered the field of competitive sports. *He* was ready for the ordeal. I wasn't. I thought he still looked sort of newly hatched and terribly vulnerable.

"Today I have to stay after school again and practice track," he announced one day, in a voice surprisingly deep for such a small boy. "Why don't you come watch me?"

Of course, I went. I watched, and my heart ached because he was trying so hard with such discouraging results. He ran with desperation, his thin legs churning furiously. Other boys ran more easily and went faster.

"I'm not too good at track," he acknowledged after several weeks of this. "I think I'll try out for the Little League. Maybe I'm the kind of boy who's good at baseball."

He wasn't. For one thing, he couldn't see the ball. He was nearsighted, even *with* glasses. He just wasn't baseball material. And each evening he returned to me exhausted and discouraged.

One night he seemed even lower than usual. His unruly brown hair stuck out in little sweaty points, and drops of perspiration had made muddy trails through the dust on his forehead. "I missed every fly that came my way," he said. "And I struck out twice."

"That's too bad," I sympathized. "Maybe you'll do better tomorrow."

He shook his head, doubtfully. I put a comforting hand on his shoulder, but he pulled away.

It isn't easy being a boy, I learned. But there were good moments — like the day I picked him up from practice and he had his new uniform. He ran to the car, the green-and-white uniform slung casually over his shoulder, and the smile on his face could have lighted up every baseball park in America.

"I got a uniform," he announced. "Some boys didn't get one. This was the last uniform, and the coach gave it to me. He said I'd earned it."

"Congratulations," I said.

He settled in the seat beside me with a happy sigh, and spread the uniform on his lap so that the name and number on the back could be read.

It was wonderful to see him so happy.

The bench-warming period began after that. One day I took him to baseball practice. He was wearing an orange sweatshirt and cut-off jeans. I left him and drove on to complete the day's errands, then returned to the practice field. I was a block away when I saw a small figure in an orange shirt stretched out on the field, not moving at all. Everyone was gathering around him. Somehow I managed to park the car and run across the field.

He wasn't seriously hurt. He had collided with another player. He was stunned, and his nose bled alarmingly; but after a bit of first aid he got up and walked unassisted to the car. The next day, both his eyes were black.

"You'd better not go to the game tonight," I said. "You don't look in very good shape."

"Aw, Mom," he protested, "you don't have to be in very good shape to sit on a bench."

He didn't sit on the bench that night, however. His persistence had finally got to the coach, who put him in for part of each game after that. Clearly, he was the kind of coach who cared for things other than winning. Johnny missed balls, made some wild throws and struck out, and all his mistakes were announced over the loudspeaker. The family's hearts bled as one. Then one night a crucial fly came his way. I saw the coach wince and cover his eyes. The ball sailed into

Johnny's glove — and stayed.

There was an unmistakable aura of success about him as we drove home. "Why not stop and get malts for the whole family?" he suggested grandly.

"Why not?" I agreed. After all, success is a relative thing.

At this moment, Johnny is asleep. He lies on his back, arms outstretched and limp. His baseball glove is carefully placed beside his pillow. I lean over to kiss the soft curve of his little-boy cheek, and an idea occurs to me. I think of mothers I know, mothers who sit in the stands and cheer sons who hit homers and win medals. It must be great to be the mother of a winner. But, I decide, it couldn't be half as heartwarming and tender an experience as mothering a gallant little loser.

Pat Van Buskirk

# Love, Helene

*An affectionate (and witty) Mother's Day tribute to a very special woman — "Mama."*

There is a country — I read about it once — where the local custom is that if you go to a house and praise some small possession, the owners feel obliged to offer it to you as a gift. I don't remember the name of the country; the only other place I know of with such a custom is my mother's apartment.

Knowing Mama, I have always been careful with my compliments, but that doesn't stop her. Mama senses admiration far more subtle than the spoken compliment. If she catches me staring at anything small enough to put in a grocery sack, she hands it to me as I leave. It would do no good to protest, "I was merely staring at that photograph of Mt. Hood because I have one exactly like it in my living room." Mama would only nod and say, "Of course. You were thinking how nice it would be to have a set. If a mother doesn't understand, who does?"

Sometimes, while visiting Mama and trying not to say or do anything complimentary, I reflect on what might have been. I have visions of her in the White House, bidding her dinner guests farewell: "Here you are, Mr. Prime Minister, that nice picture of George Washington you were admiring so much, from the Blue Room. No, take it, you like it — what do I need it for?"

Being with Mama is different, like watching an Alfred Hitchcock movie: I never know what's going to happen next. For instance, I have lasting memories of childhood walks with her. Mama noticed everything we passed. We had to stop to admire a nice house, a nice tree, a nice flower.

Mama regarded the people we saw (those who didn't look like her relatives) as portraits in a museum — no matter if people stared back. "She was pretty once, but has seen tragedy," Mama would whisper, or, "Such a handsome man, but conceited to the core." Her sharpest epithet was "Minky," reserved for the type of woman Mama thought would wear a mink to the supermarket.

As far back as I can remember, Mama was telling people they were in the wrong line of work, and suggesting alternative careers. If the landlord fixed the sink, she told him he should have been a plumber. If he couldn't fix it, Mama would wait until the plumber came and then tell him he should have been a landlord. And if either one of them told her a joke while he was putting his tools away, Mama would have to know why he hadn't gone into show business.

My turn was to come, when I grew up and became a housewife. "You missed your calling," Mama sighs, examining the doodles on my phone book. "You should have been an artist." Later, I tell her how I returned rancid fish to the supermarket and demanded a refund, and she amends this to "lawyer." I know it's horsefeathers, but I like it.

"You missed *your* calling," I tell Mama. "You should have been a vocational counselor."

"I know," she sighs. "But that's life. Maybe now that it's spring. . ."

According to Mama, there is no problem that will not be a little bit solved by the coming of spring. I grew up believing that there was only one correct way to end a discussion of things unpleasant or troublesome: nod at the calendar, pat somebody on the back if possible, and sigh, "Maybe in the spring. . ."

I could understand how certain problems — sinus conditions, chapped lips, sticking windows — would be expected to respond to the change of seasons. But I never tried to unravel the spring magic that Mama vowed would help me understand fractions or long division.

I was not the only target of Mama's philosophy. At one time or another, Mama had several dozen people in the neighborhood waiting for spring to relieve them of indigestion, mice, domestic difficulties, and trouble with the horizontal hold on their television sets.

Sometimes, sitting in school during history (which Mama promised me I'd find less boring in the spring), I would daydream my mother into other places and other times. Once I saw her patting Napoleon on the back, after he got the news from the Russian front. ("Wait. Maybe in spring. . .") She was beside George Washington at Valley Forge, brushing snow off his epaulets. ("In spring, maybe, you'll win the Revolution. I wouldn't worry about it.") She was looking over Edison's shoulder, comforting him in his early failures. ("Don't worry, maybe in the spring you'll try something new. Everything will be all right.")

I have been worrying for weeks now about what to give my mother for Mother's Day. For most people this is a modest problem, solved by the purchase of a bathrobe or a box of candy. For me, however, Mother's Day represents an annual challenge to do the impossible — find a gift that will make neither Mama nor me feel terrible.

Expensive gifts — which Mama defines as costing over $1.98 — are out, because they make Mama feel terrible. ("This is awful," she says, examining an apron. "I feel just terrible. You shouldn't have spent the money on me.") Inexpensive presents — under $1.98 — please Mama, but they make *me* feel terrible.

There is always the danger a gift given to Mama will bounce swiftly back to the giver. If I buy her something wearable she perceives in an instant that it could be let in here, let out there, and it would fit me perfectly. If I give her a plant, she cuts off the top for me to take home and root in a glass of water. If I give her something edible, she wants me to stay for lunch and eat it.

Papa, a sensible man, long ago stopped trying to shop for

Mama. Instead, on Mother's Day, her birthday and other appropriate occasions, he composes for her a short epic poem in which he tells of their meeting, courtship and subsequent marriage. After nearly 30 years of poems, Papa sometimes worries that the edge of his poetic inspiration has dulled, but Mama doesn't complain. She comes into the room while he is struggling over a gift poem and says, "It doesn't have to rhyme, as long as it's from the heart."

This year, finally, I think I too have found a painless gift for Mama. I am going to give her a magazine article, unrhymed but from the heart, in which I wish her "Happy Mother's Day," and tell her that there's nothing Papa or I could ever buy, find or make for her that would be half good enough, anyway.

Helene Melyan

*While my mother believes in the Golden Rule, she also advocates a second maxim, which she terms her Iron Rule: "Don't do for others what they wouldn't take the trouble to do for themselves."*

Mrs. D. Fulton

# Mama Was An Ecologist

*A light look at a resourceful woman.*

What poor as well as rich families leave on the sidewalks these days for the Sanitation Department to cart away looks to me like the stuff people used to load on moving vans, not on dump trucks. I see lamps, umbrellas, TV sets, playpens, baby carriages, bicycles, tables, refrigerators — all cut down in the prime of life.

We have been educated to use; we shall now have to be re-educated to reuse, restore, renew and conserve.

My mother was a specialist in the resourceful use of resources. She did not know words like ecology, recycling, reprocessing. She knew only that if you don't take care of what you have, you won't have it. The methods Mama used may themselves be reusable today. Sometimes out of necessity, but just as often out of sheer ingenuity, Mama invented uses for things which their inventors had never thought of. "If you don't have an education," she would say, "you have to use your head."

She put everything to work for her: A little castor oil would make anything go faster — clocks, fans, drills, or kids; a brand-new toilet plunger stuck on the bathroom wall near the sink made a great towel rack; a few drops of camphor oil in a gas-steam iron and you could press a shirt and cure a cough at the same time; a pair of pants under the mattress at bedtime guaranteed a sharp crease (perhaps four or five of them) by morning; still-warm laundry water was good for washing the floor, or spilling out of the window on those noisy kids outside; a wedding ring was good for cracking nuts, knocking on steam pipes, prying the cap off a soda bottle, or tapping a kid on the cranium to get his attention;

flour and water made paste, plaster or pancakes; an old bagel made a first-class teething ring; and bread never got stale if you had more children.

A hairpin could be used for opening door locks, scratching heads, pulling frazzled shoelaces through, untying knots, extracting coins from piggy banks, cleaning wax out of candlesticks or ears, turning a screw, repairing a watch, pulling a corset together, plucking a chicken, and most important, as a tool for extracting other hairpins from drains. If the hairpins didn't do the trick a button hook could be used. If the button hook went down the drain Mama used a hairpin on a string to fish it out. If *both* went down the drain, you fished them out with a straightened-out wire coat hanger.

We kids discovered on our own that: used razor blades could be resharpened by honing them against the inside surface of a glass; a burnt match could be lit from a lighted gas burner to light an unlighted burner, then reused for drawing beards on ladies' pictures in the newspaper, or darkening our adolescent mustaches before going out on a date; a shoe box could be turned into a lunch box, or a model home subdivided into four or five fully furnished rooms, or a movie house with the light projected from a cut-out square at the rear, or a home for a turtle, or a bed for a doll, or just a box marked "Private. Keep out. This means you."

Food was thrown in, not out. Each of us functioned like a garbage pail. Mama stepped on your foot, you opened your mouth, in went something, and you flipped your lid.

"There is no such thing as bad food," Mama used to say. "There are only spoiled-rotten children."

"Ma, I'm hungry."

"Take a piece of bread and butter."

"I don't want bread and butter."

"If you don't want bread and butter you're not hungry."
Next case!

An empty milk bottle was not really empty until it had been partially refilled with water and shaken to release the milky coating which was then drunk as milk. Hot water poured into an empty ketchup bottle could provide a pretty good bowl of tomato soup. A smear of mustard between two pieces of rye bread made a mouth-watering corned-beef sandwich.

For me, Mama's methods die hard. When visiting people's homes, I still cannot get myself to use one of the nice clean guest towels piled up neatly on the flushameter tank. I look for an old one behind the door, and if I don't find it, I use the inside of the shower curtain. My conscience is clean: "I didn't start a fresh towel, Ma."

Sam Levenson

*Mother had ten children, and a friend asked her how she divided her love between so many. "You don't divide," replied Mother. "You multiply."*

Mrs. S.G. Brown

# The Twenty-Year Secret

You hear a lot about kids fooling their mothers, but you hardly ever hear of a mother fooling her kids. But I knew one who did. Mine. But in the end we found out the truth about her.

We grew up during the Depression. The Depression meant no shoes, no meat and barely enough shelter — with a fighting chance that the whole family would be evicted onto the sidewalk. That was the Depression. And it was harder still because my father had left us.

Well, all through those grim years my mother managed to keep her four children fed, sheltered, clothed and in school. Her hair turned white before she was 35. She was cheerful enough, but her eyes had a sort of haunted look. She never had any pretty clothes or good times.

When we four kids grew up, we all did well enough to pool a fairly handsome hunk of cash to send Mom each week, so that whatever years she had left from about 50 on would be different from the years before. But we were all kind of disappointed in Mom's new life. She didn't move into a new home; she said she was perfectly comfortable in the old one. She didn't hire any help to take her off her feet; she said she liked doing housework. She didn't buy any pretty clothes. She kept delaying the vacations to Florida or to Europe that we planned for her — until we gave up planning. Still, that weekly check came in, and, as we four figured it, since she didn't spend more than a fraction of it each week she must have saved a considerable amount by the time she died, some 20 years later.

Well, when we went through her papers we found out that Mom was broke! Those checks had been spent the instant they arrived. On what? As soon as we kids were off her back, Mom had secretly arranged with a refugee outfit to ship her four war orphans from Europe. She'd set them up in a home near hers, and for 20 years she'd educated them, seen them through sickness and teen-age problems, and, in two cases, into marriage.

She never told us about the four new kids. I guess she wasn't sure we'd approve of her going through the whole mess all over again. I'm not sure we would have, either. You see, it isn't easy for kids who've grown up seeing their mothers knock themselves out half their lives to raise them to understand that motherhood is a sort of incurable condition.

Al Capp

# THE
# LIGHTER
# SIDE

# What Is A Mother?

The search for identity, once an exclusive concern of adolescents and college students, now preoccupies Mother as well. Busily serving her community, helping her husband, and — above all — molding her children into healthy, happy, productive citizens, she increasingly stops to ask, "But who am I?"

In attempts to answer her, psychiatrists have explored her id, polls have surveyed her attitudes, sociologists have written learned reports, foundations have set aside large sums of money to investigate her "role." Even a President of the United States has set up a Commission on the Status of Women.

Here, the question is put to the people who have the answers. We are pleased to present a view of Mother by those who keep her under closest surveillance and probably know her best — her children.

*Who is a Mother? She knows what is important. That is why God asked them to be a mother.*

*Lizann*

*A mother is the only one if she sings your favorite song it stop thundering*

*Louise*

*A Mother doesnt' do anything exsept she wants to. Nobody maks her take baths and naps or takes away her frog.*

*Gary*

*Mothers get mad if you use your brothers toothbrush but he doesn't care.*

*Larry*

*If I forget to tell my mother I need my shepherd costume tomorrow morning, she finds one in the night. That is a mother!*

*Harry*

*Mothers are wonderful! She spends all her time on you. A mother is just like God except God is better.*

*Laura*

*It is lucky that we have a mother because if we did not have a mother everything would be in a big big mess.*

*Fred T.*

*Mothers are people with X-ray eyes. They always know where you are, what you are doing, how your doing it, who your doing it with and where your doing it. They are the first ones to find out what you don't want anyone to know.*

*Jack*

*What a mother is. A very dear person who has given up her life with her parents to be by herself with her husband. Also to raise a few children herself.*

*Hester*

*A Mother is a person too.*

*David*

Compiled by Lee Parr McGrath and
Joan Scobey

# See Mother Run

*Here comes the yellow school bus. Hurry, children, hurry!*

See Mother. Mother is sleeping. "Jump up, Mother," says Father. "Jump up! Today is the first day of school!"

Oh, see Mother get out of bed! Her eyes are not open. Her slippers are on the wrong feet. She cannot find the bedroom door. Funny Mother!

"Hurry, children," says Mother. "Today is the first day of school!"

See the children go down to the kitchen. They hurry slowly on the first day of school, don't they? Mother hurries to the kitchen, too. Mother has one eye open now.

"I will give you a good breakfast," says Mother. "I will give you juice, porridge, toast, bacon, eggs, and milk from the friendly cow."

"Euchh!" says Laurie.

"Euchh!" says Bobby.

"Euchh!" says Chris.

Laurie wants cottage cheese and tea. Bobby wants Choko-Krunch Korn Krisps and Cocoa with marshmallow. Chris wants three bananas.

*"Euchh!"* says Mother.

Here comes Father. He is wearing his clean white shirt and good brown suit. Father is an executive.

"I am going to work, Mother," says Father. "May I please have a dollar to put in my pocket?"

"I do not have a dollar, Father," says Mother. "Ask the children. The children have many dollars."

The children give Father a dollar. How good they are! "Good-by! Good-by, Father!" call Laurie, Bobby, Chris and Mother. Father waves good-by. Father is glad he is an executive and not a mother.

"Children, children!" says Mother. "Hurry and put on your clothes. Hurry, hurry! Soon the school bus will come!"

See Laurie. Laurie is combing her hair. See Bobby. Bobby is reading about Willie Mays. See Chris. Chris is tattooing his stomach with a ballpoint pen.

See Mother's hair stand up! What is Mother saying? Those words are not in our book, are they? *Run, children, run!*

"Mother, Mother!" says Laurie. "I have lost a shoe!"

"Mother, Mother!" says Bobby. "I think I am sick. I think I may throw up on the yellow school bus!"

"Mother, Mother!" says Chris. "My zipper is stuck, and I have a jelly bean in my ear!"

Oh, see Mother run!

"I am going mad," says Mother. "Here is Laurie's shoe on the stove. Here are other pants for Chris. Here is a thermometer for Bobby, who does not look sick to me." Now what are the children doing?

Laurie is combing her hair. Bobby is playing the banjo. Chris is under the bed feeding jelly beans to the cat.

"Oh!" says Mother. "Hurry, hurry! It is time for the yellow school bus!"

Mother is right. (Mother is *always* right.) Here comes the yellow school bus!

See all the children on the bus jump up and down. Jump! Jump! Jump! See the pencil boxes fly out the windows! Listen to the driver of the yellow school bus. He cannot yell as loud as the children, can he? Run, Laurie! Run, Bobby! Run, Chris!

See Mother throw kisses. Why do Laurie, Bobby and Chris pretend they do not know Mother?

"Good-by! Good-by!" calls Mother.

*"Barrooom!"* goes the yellow bus.

How quiet it is.
Here is Chris's sweater in the boot box.
Here are Bobby's glasses under the cat.
Here is Laurie's comb in the fruit bowl.

57

Here is crunchy cereal all over the kitchen floor.

Here is Mother. Crunch, crunch, crunch. Mother is pouring a big cup of coffee. Mother is sitting down.

Mother does not say anything.

Mother does not do anything.

Mother just sits and smiles.

Why is Mother smiling?

Joan Mills

# *Out Of The Mouths Of Babes . . .*

*As a single parent with small children, I returned to work having the usual guilt feelings about leaving them while they were so young. I assured my children, however, that they could call me at the office whenever they had a problem.*

*One day my four-year-old daughter called and said that she had to speak with me. "Mommy," she said, "my goldfish died." This was exactly the kind of situation I feared would happen — she wanted comforting, and I was in the middle of an important meeting.*

*"Honey," I began, as everyone in the meeting listened, "I know this is a hard time for you, but I'm very busy right now. As soon as I get home we'll have a long talk about it. Okay?"*

*"But, Mommy," she pleaded, "I have to ask you a question now."*

*The meeting could wait! My child needed me. "Go ahead, dear. Ask your question."*

*"Mommy, would it be all right if we eat him for supper?"*

*Betty L. Hagerty*

# How To Drive Mom Crazy In The Car

Insist that you don't have to go to the bathroom. If your mother points out that sometimes you think you don't have to go and then it turns out that you do, say that you are sure. When she suggests that you try anyway, claim that you just went. Then have this conversation with your sister:

"Dibs on the front seat."

"You had it last time."

"No, I didn't. *You* had it last time."

"Did not."

"Did too."

"Did not."

"Did too. Mom, I want the front seat; she had it last time. I get it, don't I?"

Your mother will say that she can't stand it another minute — no one is sitting in front. Sit on the hood above the headlights, waiting to leave. Then announce that you intend to sit next to the window. That's no problem, your mother will explain, since there are two windows — you and your sister can each have one. Discuss windows with your sister:

"I want that window."

"I want it."

"You got it last time."

"*You* got it."

"Did not. You make me barf. I bet you eat worms."

"Mo-om! He said I eat worms."

Now your mother will point out that if she hears one more word, neither of you is going anywhere. As you get into the car, mumble, "Good, I don't want to go." Then tell your sister to stay on her own side. Show her where her side begins: Draw an imaginary line down the back of the front seat, across the floor, and up the back seat. Tell her not to cross the line. Say, "Stay on your own side — I don't want your cooties."

Shortly after the car leaves the driveway, announce that you have to go to the bathroom and deny kicking your sister. Agree to hold it for a while, and when she kicks you back, kick her again. While she cries, explain to your mom that you wouldn't have kicked your sister if she hadn't kicked you first. Your mother will say, "Cut it out, both of you, or I'll stop the car right here." Then she will slow down the car and ask if that's what you want. After that, she will say that you should each stay on your own side.

Read a comic. Pay no attention when your mother points out interesting things to see. Ask if you are almost there yet. Declare that you have to go real bad. As soon as the car pulls into a gas station, run. Afterward, ask to stop for ice cream.

Prop up your feet on the window ledge so that people driving by can see them. Ask to stop for ice cream. Ask if you are almost there yet. Then start to sing at the top of your lungs . . .

"I can't stand it! Stop it! I can't stand it another minute!"

Deny that you are the person kicking the seat.

Be engrossed looking out the window while you casually move your hand on the seat over to your sister's side. If she doesn't notice, poke your pinky into her leg. Then she will say for sure, "You're on my side. Get off. Ma, he's on my side." Remove hand, say that you were not, look out window, put hand back, and leave it there until she hits you. Hit her back. While she cries as she yells, "Stop hitting me," and hits you back, yell, "You hit me first." Kick the seat when you miss kicking her. Knock your head against the door and cry.

At this point, start listening to your mother as she finishes what she began saying after the first hit: "Stop it, both of you. I've had enough. You hear me? If either of you lays a finger on the other, if I hear one more word out of either of you, that's it. Understood? I'm never taking you anywhere again. Is that what you want? Is it? I swear — if I hear one more peep, I'm turning around."

Sniffle. Wipe your nose on the back of your hand. Sniffle again. Lean back against the seat. Sniffle. Close your eyes: You are now riding in the back seat of a chauffeur-driven limousine with a TV — all alone. Think about your sister. Open your eyes and look at her. She is so disgusting. Sniffle. Wipe your nose on your sleeve. Look out the window. Wonder if you're almost there yet.

Delia Ephron

# Boys Will Be Boys . . .

On the Merv Griffin TV show, in an exchange about embarrassing moments, Jack Ford, son of former President Gerald Ford, remembered a visit to the White House by Queen Elizabeth of England.

"I was all excited and anxious to meet her," Ford recalled. "Hurrying to get into my formal clothes, I could not find dress studs for my shirt and rushed to Dad's room to look for some.

"Having no luck there, I ran down the hall and pressed the elevator button to return to my room. As the elevator opened and I stepped in with my dress shirt unfastened, I found myself with the Queen, Prince Philip, and my mother and dad. As Mother turned to introduce me, the Queen simply said, 'I have one just like that!'"

*Merv Griffin*

# In Mother We Trust

A woman in an out-of-town station wagon arrived at the zoo in Washington, D.C., with her four young children and their dog, only to learn that dogs were not allowed in the zoo. Reluctant to leave their new and valued pet alone in the car, she told the two older children to visit the zoo while she stayed with the younger ones and the dog; then when they returned, she would take the little ones in. As they were talking, an elderly woman standing nearby spoke up: "Why don't you go in with the four children and leave the dog with me? I'll sit in the car with him till you get back."

The young mother hesitated, for it seemed chancy to leave the dog with a stranger. The woman smiled understandingly. "Would it help you to know," she asked, "that I am Walter Cronkite's mother?"

It did — and the trip to the zoo was a success.

*Miriam Young*

# My Wild Irish Mother

I'm never going to write my autobiography, and it's all my mother's fault. I don't hate her, so I have practically no material. In fact, the situation is worse than I'm pretending. We are crazy about her — and you know I'll never get a book out of that.

Mother was born Kitty O'Neill, in Kinsale, Ireland, with bright red hair, bright blue eyes, and the firm conviction that it was wrong to wait for an elevator if you were only going up to the fifth floor. It's not just that she won't wait for elevators; I have known her to reproach herself for missing one section of a revolving door.

Once, when we missed a train from New York to Washington, I fully expected her to pick up our suitcases and announce, "Well, darling, the exercise will be good for us."

When I have occasion to mutter about the financial problems involved in maintaining five children in a large house, Mother is quick to get to the root of the problem. "Remember," she says, "you take cabs a lot." In Mother's opinion, an able-bodied woman is perfectly justified in taking a taxi to the hospital if her labor pains are closer than ten minutes apart.

The youngest daughter of wealthy and indulgent parents, Mother was sent to finishing schools in France and to the Royal Conservatory of Music in London. When she came to America to marry my father, her only qualifications as housewife and mother were the ability to speak four languages, play three musical instruments and make blanc-mange.

I, naturally, wasn't around during those first troubled months when Mother learned to cook. But my father can still recall the day she boiled corn, a delicacy unknown in Ireland at that time, for five hours until the cobs were tender.

To her four children — all low-metabolism types, inexplicably — Mother's energy has always seemed awesome. "What do you think?" she's prone to say. "Do I have time to cut the grass before I stuff the turkey?" But her whirlwind activity is potentially less dangerous than her occasional moments of repose. Then she sits, staring into space, clearly lost in languorous memories. The fugitive smile that hovers about her lips suggests the gentle melancholy of one hearing Mozart played beautifully. Suddenly she leaps to her feet. "I know it will work," she says. "All we have to do is remove that wall, plug up the windows and extend the porch."

It's fortunate that she has the thrust and energy of a well-guided missile or she wouldn't get a lick of work done, because everybody who comes to her house, even to read the gas meter, always stays at least an hour. I used to think that they were all beguiled by her Irish accent, but I have gradually gleaned that they are telling her the story of their invariably unhappy lives.

"Do you remember my lovely huckleberry man?" Mother will ask. "Oh, yes, you do — he had red hair and ears. Well, his brother-in-law sprained his back and hasn't worked in six months, and we're going to have to take a bundle of clothes over to those children." Or again, "Do you remember that nice girl in the Scranton Dry Goods? Oh, yes, you do — she was in lampshades, and she had gray hair and wore gray dresses. Well, she's having an operation next month, and you must remember to pray for her."

Mother's credo, by the way, is that if you want something, anything, don't just sit there — pray for it. And she combines a Job-like patience in the face of the mysterious ways of the Almighty with a flash of Irish rebellion which will bring her to say — and I'm sure she speaks for many of us — "Jean, what I am really looking for is a blessing that's not in disguise."

She has a knack of penetrating disguises, whether it be small boys who claim that they have taken baths or middle-aged daughters who swear that they have lost five pounds. She also has a way of cutting things to size. Some time ago I had a collection of short pieces brought out in book form, and I sent one of the first copies to her. Her delight fairly bubbled off the pages of the letter. "Darling," she wrote, "isn't it marvelous the way those old pieces of yours finally came to the surface like a dead body!"

One of the most charming things about Mother was the extraordinary patience with which she would allow us youngsters to "instruct" her. While she knew a great deal about such "useless" things as music and art and literature, she knew nothing whatever, we discovered as we were growing up, about isosceles triangles or watts and volts or the Smoot-Hawley tariff. We, of course, made haste to repair these gaps.

I discovered recently just how much of this unrelated information has stayed with her. I was driving her to a train when she noticed a squirrel poised on a wire that ran between two five-story buildings. "Look at that little squirrel way up on that wire," she said. "You know, if he gets one foot on the ground he'll be electrocuted."

But if Mother's knowledge of electricity is a little sketchy, there is nothing sketchy about her knowledge of any subject in which she develops an interest. About twenty years ago, when my husband and I became involved in the theater, Mother's lifelong fascination with things theatrical came to the fore. A revue we had written had just opened, and she made me promise that I would send her all the newspaper reviews, special delivery, as soon as they appeared.

In those days there were eight metropolitan dailies, and our only seriously negative notice appeared in *The Sun*. Ward Morehouse was then the critic on *The Sun;* but he was out of town, and the review was written by his assistant, or, as I was willing to suppose, his office boy. So, with that special brand of feminine logic that will in the end drive my husband out of his mind, I decided to omit this particular notice in the batch I sent to Mother. This was a serious miscalculation on my part, as I realized when I got Mother's two-word telegram. It read, "Where's Morehouse?"

I knew when I started this that all I could do was list some of the things Mother does and says, because it's not possible, really, to describe her. All my life I have heard people break off their lyrical descriptions of her and announce helplessly, "You'll just have to meet her."

However, I recognize, if I cannot describe, the lovely festive air she always brings with her, so that she can arrive any old day in July and suddenly it seems to be Christmas Eve and the children seem handsomer and better behaved and all the adults seem more charming and . . .

Well, you'll just have to meet her.

Jean Kerr

# Why Mothers Don't Get Sick

There is a time of year when everyone gets what is known as the "24-hour bug." The one thing clear about the 24-hour bug is that *nobody* has it for exactly 24 hours.

Children can stretch the disease into three full days off from school, during which their mothers bring them meals on a tray and permit them to look at all the awful daytime television shows. One of the nicest things that can happen to a child is to get the bug that's going around.

Fathers enjoy it, too. They don't have it quite so long, but they have it louder. Mothers, however, can catch, suffer and recover from the 24-hour bug in a flat 12 hours. Surely this is a medical miracle of some kind. We examine now a typical case of a typical mother who contracts a typical bug.

The first thing worth noting is that mothers react differently from other people to the first signs of fever. Children may weep, fathers get irritable. But the typical mother's reaction is pure, unadulterated joy. She *yearns* to be a little bit sick. She almost never is.

However, once in a long while she's lucky and, to her definite joy, the thermometer shows a fever. Let's assume that this fine moment comes just after lunchtime. The children are at school, the baby is napping, there's no reason why she can't get into bed immediately. All she has to do first is mix the meat loaf for supper, leave a note for the laundry-man, find a substitute for the coffee committee that night, put in the next load of wash, carry out the trash and then . . . and then go upstairs and . . . sink . . . into . . . bed. Ah-h-h-h-h! Her aching legs soak up comfort from the cool sheets, and her eyes, which have started to burn a bit, slowly, pleasurably, close. She's asleep — in the middle of the day!

Then, too soon, the front door bangs wildly open as the children explode home from school. Their cries of "Mom! *Mom!* Where ARE you?" entirely drown out her weak answering calls, but their search is determined and very shortly they appear, reacting in their several ways to the unbelievable fact that Mother is in bed.

"Didn't you *even get up yet?*" cries the younger girl, ignoring the fact that Mom obviously was up through the breakfast bedlam.

"But how am I going to get to Bill's!" — asks the boy, lurching in despair onto the bottom of the bed.

"If you're sick, what'll we have for dinner?" inquires the oldest, cutting right to the essential problem.

The point is that children are not really the unfeeling monsters they appear to be under these circumstances. It's just that the whole concept of a mother in bed, not attending to duties, is outside their picture of the way things are. A wise woman, at such a time, will play shamelessly on their sense of the dramatic. She must throw her head back against the pillow, look pale and wan, and issue tense, whispered commands.

"I'm sick," she must say clearly. "I can't do *anything*. I'll just have to leave everything to you." Then, letting her voice trail off dramatically, but careful to mention every necessary duty, she murmurs, "Cook the potatoes. . .take care of the baby. . .set the table. . ." So convincing a display of crisis will cause most children to rise nobly to the challenge, and for a time she will be left to the quiet of her room and the ache in her head.

But then Father comes home. Having received a breathless medical report from the children, he bounds into the bedroom without taking off his coat, drops heavily on the side of the bed and reaches for her hand.

"The kids say you feel terrible. Have you called Dr. Murphy? Should I go pick up the prescription? What did he say was the matter?" Suddenly she feels terribly guilty, and struggles to switch from acting sicker than she is to acting much better than she feels.

"It's nothing, darling — just this bug that's going around. I can get up and do dinner and . . ." He shakes his head firmly.

"You stay right there. Don't worry about a thing. The kids and I will take over." He sounds confident, but as she looks up at him in his rumpled business suit, with end-of-the-day fatigue in his eyes, she feels a tearful remorse.

Her room is quiet again. And empty. Her lovely languor has left. She feels scratchy and hot in the wrinkled sheets. She lies very still, straining for family sounds, feeling left out, feeling *terrible*. But everybody else seems to feel great. There seems, in fact, to be some sort of party going on, with giggling from the children and guffaws from Father, all against the clatter of plates and silverware.

Suddenly there is a dreadful crash, followed by Father's voice telling everyone loudly to get the baby out of the way for goodness sake before he cuts himself, and where is the broom, and whatever they do they must not disturb their mother. "DON'T DISTURB YOUR MOTHER," he bawls from the kitchen, making the curtains move gently up in her bedroom.

Now the house grows quiet, and it is clear to her that the family is eating dinner, while she lies there motionless, forgotten, miserable. She is not surprised that no one has thought to bring dinner to her. They've obviously forgotten about her entirely. They're obviously doing *fine* without her. There's no point in going on living.

And then there is the lovely sound of another appalling crash, and the next-to-smallest child races in breathlessly to announce, "They dropped your tray and the dog licked up all your dinner."

She dashes off and there is another period of confusing noises until, finally, all the children appear, beaming. They bring: a glass of water that has spilled over onto the tray; a plate with three beans, a cold boiled potato, a tiny slab of burned meat loaf — and themselves. "Can we come up with you while you eat? Dad's kind of mad, and it's all messy in the kitchen, and nobody knows where the broom is. Is it all right if we stay here while you eat?"

Suddenly she feels marvelous! As the children watch carefully, she eats up everything in sight, assures them that dinner was delicious, and then stretches luxuriously, noticing without surprise that the vague aches and pains she felt are gone, and only a deep, marvelous, sleepy feeling remains. The children leap up alertly, solicitously, at this sign. "Go to sleep now, Mom," they chorus. And the oldest adds, soberly, "Get better. It's no fun when you're sick."

Again the room is empty, but now it hums with comfort, and she drops into a dreamless sleep. She stirs when her husband comes in. "Go back to sleep," he says quietly. "Hope you feel better tomorrow."

And that is the great miracle. She *is* better in the morning. In fact, when she swings her legs experimentally over the side of the bed and eases to her feet, she discovers to her enormous joy that she feels great.

"I'm all better," she says exultantly to her man.

"It's about time," he replies succinctly.

And it *is* about time. Because some people have the 24-hour bug for 72 hours, and some have it for 48. But a mother, if she feels needed enough, can get over it in 12.

Joyce Lubold

# A Child's Garden Of Manners

Have you noticed a strange thing about etiquette books? They are all written for grownups. *Us.*

I don't understand it. Most adults have lovely manners. Ask an adult to hand you your glasses: he doesn't put them behind his back and say, "Guess which hand." And when you give him a birthday present he doesn't burst into tears and say, "I already *have* Chinese checkers!" What I wish is that Emily Post and Amy Vanderbilt and the others would get to work on the real trouble area — people under 12.

I know that small children have a certain animal magnetism. People kiss them a lot. But are they really in demand, socially? Are they sought after? If you have any doubts about the matter, ask yourself one question. When, by some accident, you find yourself at a large party with children present, do you just naturally gravitate to where the little ones are playing Indian Spy under the table? See what I mean? These kids need help — and direction.

In the absence of any definitive book on the subject, and inspired by passion for public service, I would like to make random suggestions.

*Table manners for children.* The first point to be established is that one sits on the chair in such a way that all four legs touch the floor at the same time. (All four legs of the chair, that is; children only *seem* to have four legs.) For children who will rock and tilt anyway, I suggest instilling in them a sense of *noblesse oblige,* so that when they go crashing back onto their heads they go bravely and gallantly and without pulling the tablecloth, the dinner and a full set of dishes with them.

The child of good manners will not use his fork to (a) comb

his hair, (b) punch holes in the tablecloth, or (c) remove buttons from his jacket. Nor will he ever, under any circumstances, place the tines of the fork under a full glass of milk and beat on the handle with a spoon.

Finally, children should be made to understand that no matter how repellent they find a given vegetable, they may not stuff large handfuls of it into their pockets. This sorry practice not only deprives the child of many necessary vitamins but frequently exposes him to intemperate criticism and even physical violence.

*Peaceful co-existence with other children.* Children should not hit each other on the head with ice skates, or telephones, or geography books. It ought to go without saying that polite children never push each other down the stairs, but I'm not sure that it does. When she was four years old, my niece, Karen, pushed her baby sister down the back stairs. After her mother had rescued the victim she flew at the oppressor and shouted, "What's the matter with you? You can't push Joanie down the stairs!" Karen listened carefully, all innocence and interest, and finally said. "I can't? How come?"

Parenthetical note to parents: In trying to keep older children from doing physical damage to their juniors, it is probably not advisable to adopt the tit-for-tat type of punishment ("If you pull Billy's hair again, I'm going to pull *your* hair!") The danger is that you may be forced into an impossible retaliation. (You can't really spit in the child's milk.) Personally, I'm in favor of generalized threats like, "If you make that baby cry once more, I'll clip you." This is open to a variety of interpretations and leaves you free to inflict such punishment as you are up to at the moment.

*Respect for the feelings of others.* One of the reasons children are such duds socially is that they say things like, "When do you think you're going to be dead, Grandma?"

It is not to be expected that a small child can be taught never to make a personal remark. But there is a time and a place. For instance, the moment Mother is all dressed up in her new blue chiffon and doesn't look a day older than 25 — well, 28 — is *not* the time for Gilbert to ask, "Why do you have all those stripes on your forehead, Mommy?"

Children should realize that parents are emotionally insecure, and that there are times when they need loving-kindness. Unfortunately, a relationship with a child, like any love affair, is complicated by the fact that the two parties almost never feel the same amount of ardor at the same time. The day you're flying to Athens (for two weeks) and you're filled with terrible foreboding that you may never see the little darlings again, you can hardly round them up to say good-by. And, when you do locate one of them, he scarcely looks up from his work. "Darling," you say, "aren't you going to say good-by and give me a *good* kiss? I'm going to be gone for two whole weeks." "Sure," he says. " 'By, Mom. Can I have a Coke?"

*Respect for the property of others.* Children should bear in mind that, no matter how foolish it seems, adults become attached to material objects like typewriters, wrist watches and car keys. I am working without statistics here, but I do have the feeling, too, that we wouldn't have so many broken homes if children could be made aware of the unwisdom of using their fathers' fountain pens to punch holes in evaporated milk cans.

Just as there are animals that kill prey they have no intention of eating, so there are children who take things they have no way of using. It may be reprehensible, but it is at least understandable that a child should take a sterling silver gravy ladle to the beach: it's almost as good to dig with as a sand shovel. But why do they take meat thermometers, or the little knobs off the tops of lamp shades? Sometimes when you investigate what seems to be meaningless mayhem, you find that there is a certain idiotic logic behind the whole thing. When, for instance, I found one of the smaller boys unfurling a roll of toilet paper out the attic window, it turned out that he was merely trying to discover how long a roll of toilet paper really is. I can understand that, sort of.

There are times, of course, when it's hard to know just what to say. Last winter I found on the breakfast table a letter addressed to Mommy Kerr. It was on my very best stationery, and there were ten brand-new stamps (mine) plastered on the envelope. The message read:

*Dear Mommy: John is mad at you because you won't let us put our snowballs in the freezer but I am not mad at you because I love you.*

*Your friend,*

*Colin*

Well, there you are. When you get right down to it, it was worth 10 stamps.

Jean Kerr

*A friend of mine who had her hands full with four young children was taken aback one day when her husband brought home a gift — a young, frisky puppy. Her children were all excited and asked her what they should name the pup. "Better call it Mother," she said, "because if that dog stays, I'm going!"*

Felix Hower

# Pen Names

*Returning to college when one's own children are in grade school creates certain problems, such as competition for ball-point pens. Thus, I have taken to buying large quantities of cheap pens and scratching the owner's name onto each one. One day in speech class, the instructor surprised us with the assignment of giving an impromptu sales speech. I listened carefully to the young man who was chosen to go first. From my front-row seat, I could almost see the wheels working inside his head as he extolled the virtues of a certain brand-name pen.*

*"And wouldn't you rather have a prestige name printed on your pen," he asked rhetorically as he leaned over and picked up my obviously cheap model, "than a name like . . ." He paused, peered closer, then concluded in apparent disbelief, "Mommy?"*

*Cheryl Muller*

# MAGICAL
# MOMENTS
# AND
# MEMORIES

# The Day I Met My Mother

Mine was, at times, a solitary childhood. Born in Chung-king, China, of missionary parents, I lost my mother at birth. I was two months old when my distraught father sent me to Mother's favorite sister in Morgantown, W.Va. There I grew up in the house where Mother had spent her girlhood.

When Aunt Ruth was at home, I was surrounded by love. But she was our sole breadwinner and worked in an office six days a week. Left with a procession of hired girls, I felt the loneliness of the big, old house.

In the evenings, before Aunt Ruth came home, I often sat on the floor beneath a picture of my mother — a sweet-faced young woman of 20, with dark eyes and black curly hair. There was one question always in my mind: *What was my mother like?* If only I could have known her!

Twenty years passed. I had grown up, married and had a baby, named Lucy for her grandmother — the mother I'd so longed to know.

One spring morning, 18-month-old Lucy and I boarded a train for Morgantown to visit Aunt Ruth. A woman offered me half her seat in the crowded car.

After settling my baby in my arms for a nap, I started to talk with the woman. She said she was going to Morgantown to see her daughter and brand-new grandson. "Surely you know my aunt, Ruth Wood," I said. "She's had a real-estate office in Morgantown for years."

"No," she answered. "I've been away for a long time, and that name is not familiar to me."

For several minutes, the woman looked out the window. Then, without turning her head, she began to speak.

"There was a Miss Lucy Wood, a teacher, in Morgantown

years ago. She probably left there before you were born. I haven't thought of her for years, but once I loved her very much. She was my teacher. My parents owned a bakery on Watts Street. They were on the verge of divorce. They fought and quarreled all the time. I had to work very hard at home and in the bakery, too.

"I loved school, though I didn't make good grades. Miss Wood's room was a happy place; it seemed like heaven to me. One day, after my folks had a big fight at breakfast, I came to school late, holding back the tears. Miss Wood kept me after school. I thought she would scold me but, instead, she let me tell her my troubles. She made me feel how much my brothers and sisters, and even my parents, needed me — and from that day on, my life was worth living.

"A few months later, I heard a little girl say: 'Miss Wood's going to marry a missionary and go live in China!' I went home crying. My parents stopped in the middle of a fight to ask me what was wrong, but they could not know how great a light was going out in my life. I couldn't sleep that night.

"The next day, Miss Wood again kept me after school to see what was wrong. When I told her, she looked surprised and tender. 'Please *don't* go way off to China!' I begged.

"'Viola,' she answered, 'I can't give up China. I'm going where my heart calls me, with the man I love. But I'll think of you often, and I'll send you a postcard.'

"I'd never had any mail of my own, so that made me feel better. When I told my mother, she shook her head, saying, 'Don't feel too bad, Viola, if she forgets; she'll have so many folks to write to.'

"Two months later, I got a postcard with a picture of the Yangtze River, postmarked Chungking, China. 'Are you still making me proud of you, my little brave one?' it asked. If anyone had given me a million dollars, it couldn't have made me more proud.

"Right after that, my parents broke up and we moved away from Morgantown. I raised my five brothers and sisters, married, and raised four children of my own.

"Goodness, we are almost there! I've talked too much. I do hope I haven't bored you."

Then, for the first time, she turned to me and saw the tears in my eyes.

"Would you like to see Lucy Woods' granddaughter?" I asked. My baby was waking from her nap. My heart was singing. The burning question of my childhood had been richly answered. At long last, I knew exactly what my mother had been like.

Faith L. Mahaney

# *The Most Wonderful Words*

*I stayed with my parents for several days after the birth of our first child. One afternoon I remarked to my mother that it was surprising our baby had dark hair since both my husband and I are fair. She said, "Well, your daddy has black hair."*

*"But, Mama, that doesn't matter because I'm adopted."*

*With an embarrassed smile she said the most wonderful words I've ever heard: "I always forget."*

Rodessa E. Morris

# Perfect Moment

*Once in a lifetime there is a moment we can never for-get. . .*

Somewhere along the road between "beginning" and "ending" there is a perfect moment for every living soul. There may possibly be more than one. But for the most part we are too busy, too young, too adult, too sophisticated, too this or too that to recognize it — and so the moment may be lost.

My perfect moment came when I was eight years old. I awoke one spring night to find moonlight flooding my room through the open window. It was so bright that I sat up in bed. There was no sound at all anywhere. The air was soft and heavy with the fragrance of pear blossoms and honey-suckle.

I crept out of bed and tiptoed softly out of the house. Eight-year-olds were not supposed to be astir at this hour. But I wanted to sit in the swing for a while and watch the moonlight. As I closed the door behind me, I saw my mother sitting on the porch steps. She looked up and smiled and, putting her finger to her lips, reached out with her other hand and drew me down beside her. I sat as close as I could and she put her arm around me.

The whole countryside was hushed and sleeping; no lights burned in any house. The moonlight was liquid silver and so bright we could see the dark outline of the woods a mile away. "Isn't it beautiful?" I whispered, and Mother's arm tightened about me.

For a long time we were perfectly still. The stars were pale and far away. Now and then the moonlight would strike a leaf of the Maréchal Niel rose beside the porch and be caught for an instant in a dewdrop like a tiny living spark. The shrubs were hung with necklaces of diamonds, and the grass was sweet with the dampness.

In all this great brooding silence that seemed so infinite, the miracle of life was going on unseen and unheard. The bird sitting on her eggs in the mulberry tree carried out a divine purpose. The hills, undisturbed by passing centuries, proclaimed strength and grandeur. The moving of the stars, the planets, the countless worlds, all were governed and held within the safety of the omnipotent yet gentle hand of the Creator.

Mother pointed toward the cedar tree. "Look," she whispered softly, "that star seems caught in the branches."

As we watched it, suddenly from the topmost point of a pear tree a mockingbird burst into song. It was as though the joy that overflowed his heart must find expression. The notes were pure gold, free and clear and liquid as the moonlight, rising, falling, meltingly sweet. At times they were so soft as to be barely audible; then he would sing out, a rapturous *profondo*. As suddenly as it had begun, the concert ended and the night was silvery still again.

An eight-year-old does not analyze his thoughts, he may not even be aware that he is surrounded by infinity. But he sees a star impaled on the branch of a cedar tree, and knows pure ecstasy. He hears a mockingbird sing in the moonlight, and is filled with speechless joy. He feels his mother's arms about him, and knows complete security.

The surging, sweeping process of life, the moving of worlds and the flowing of tides, may be incomprehensible to him. But he may nevertheless be strangely aware that he has had a glimpse through an open door, and has known a perfect moment.

Gladys Bell

# Casey's Walk

*A mother rediscovers through her son the childhood magic of a summer afternoon.*

I am no mere observer anymore. I learned to participate today: participate in my son's childhood. My son and a little girl I hadn't thought of in years shook the blowsy cobwebs from a corner of my mind and led me to a wonderful awakening. I only wonder how many times in the past they called me to join them and I failed to hear.

After lunch today, six-year-old Casey lingered at the table, head propped in his hand, one catsup-tinted finger tracing circles on the cloth. There was a brooding uncertainty in his eyes.

"Nice lunch, Mom," he said.

He paused briefly, obviously summoning courage. Then, "Can we go for that walk today?" he blurted.

"That walk" was one I had been promising for . . . well, how many weeks? Two? Three?

"Not this afternoon, " I started to say, thinking of dishes in the sink, laundry waiting to be washed. But I saw the corners of his mouth tense for a downward turn, his whole body taut in a defensive set that said, "I already know the answer." And, suddenly, household chores seemed less important than honoring an oft-made, never-kept commitment.

"Not this very minute," I salvaged. "I've got to put my sweater on."

Moments later, I clutched his hand and we were off, closing one door and opening another.

The garden turned to lawn, the lawn to scrub, and at the bottom of our property a tree trunk bridged the creek. Balancing carefully, we crossed. Casey automatically threw a rock into the sun-dappled water and so, impulsively, did I. That astonished him, and he giggled. A contagious giggle that spread to me. I was beginning to enjoy this adventure.

Across the creek we entered a little copse, a woody patch. Casey's budding manhood asserted itself. "Here," he said, "you'll need a walking stick." He found me one, and we started down a path that ran beside a honeysuckle-covered, long-forgotten fence. Soon, less than 500 yards from our backyard, I was lost in a land I've never seen. Casey volunteered assurance that he knew the way.

Our path became a trail, thick with overgrowth, suggesting dismal thoughts of poison ivy and calamine lotion. Casey stopped where an upstart wind had blown a tree across a break in the fence. Stepping over the trunk, he announced proudly, "Rob and I saw a bear here yesterday!"

My tolerant adult smile must have seemed to answer, "Ridiculous," for abruptly the excitement left his eyes. His shoulders sagged as he turned and walked on, between bushes that were bending in a sudden vagrant wind. And borne on that wind from afar—not in miles but in years—came the echo of a little girl's voice: *Daddy, there must be Indians down there. I found an arrowhead with dried blood on it.* And a deep voice, warm with wonder, replying, *You did? We'd better be careful, then.*

I ran to catch up. Breathlessly I cried, "Casey, I'll bet there *are* bears here. We'd better watch out for them!"

The magic in words! Casey's eyes sparkled, his shoulders straightened. Those few words had made him feel as right, as important, as they had made me feel, years ago.

And now it was a bright new path we trod. I didn't notice the overgrowth anymore, or worry about the ivy. These woods might indeed hold bears or Indians. Or Peter Pan and Tinker Bell. In our private Never-Never-Land we were laughing and running, all three of us . . . a mother, her son, and a little girl I had rediscovered at long last. A little boy tugged at the sleeves of my sweater, and a little girl tugged at the sleeves of my heart as we searched under rocks for treasures, chased butterflies to the heights of the soaring skies, and sent ladybugs home to their threatened children. We three. We two. We one.

Just as my bones were pleading for a chance to rest, Casey called a halt and sat down on a log. With an ill-concealed sigh of relief, I joined him.

"This is where we sit and tell stories," he said. "It's a special log. Isn't it huge?"

"Yes, it is," I acknowledged. . .and meant it, though someday he'll come back as a man and find it small.

The afternoon shadows lengthened and it was time to leave. But Casey suddenly scurried off, returning with a fistful of jaded dandelions which he thrust into my hands. "I love you, Mom," he said.

The words, I knew, were not entirely for grown-up, adult me. They were for the new friend Casey had met, for the child we had both discovered in the woods. In me.

At last we started home, again. . .not three, but two of us, leaving the little girl behind on the log. There she would wait, I knew, to join us on our next adventure. Soon. For I had promised myself, and her, that she would not have to wait too long.

Judy Coffin

# To Claudia—With Love

Before Claudia reached the teen-age stage, I couldn't believe the stories mothers told me of the unpredictable way their children changed their personalities from day to day, from moment to moment, during the years of 12, 13 and 14. Claudia is now 13, and in the past year her father and I have observed this metamorphosis firsthand — usually to our utter consternation.

There are the reassuring moments, however, the quiet talks — generally at bedtime — when there are no barriers between us, no angers, no hurts. During one of these sessions recently she brought up the subject of careers.

"Is there a chance I could learn Braille, Mommy?"

"Braille? Why?"

"Well, because last year in school I used to lead Tom around, that blind boy who had a Braille machine. You remember?" Her voice is soft with the wonder of the dream. "If I knew Braille, I could have written things for him and helped him in lots of ways."

I have to blink quickly and swallow a sudden lump in my throat. This is the glorious unpredictability of teenagers. This is the same 13-year-old Claudia who is always goofing off in the senseless ways that delight comedians and cartoonists, and exasperate parents. This is the same Claudia who spends hours murmuring gibberish over the telephone, who reads books and magazines in a bubble bath, and emerges with unscrubbed arms, neck and ears that contrast eloquently with the clean body and legs that stayed beneath the suds.

I suggest gently, "Well, I'm sure the Institute for the Blind or somebody would be glad to help you learn Braille on Saturdays. Are you thinking along those lines for a career?" I remember that our Claudia always mothers the youngest children in our neighborhood, and had effortlessly taught a five-year-old to ice-skate in two hours.

Now she speaks slowly and seriously. "I want to do something to help kids," she explains. "I love the little ones — you know that — and I want to help the ones who are sick and need to learn to do things for themselves. . . ."

"You mean — rehabilitation work with crippled children?"

"Yes, something like that."

I sit beside her on the bed. She snuggles into my arm and falls into a light doze.

I remember the many pies I have baked for her Sunday-school sales. I remember all the things we've done together, how she changed my life from a self-centered one into one of many interests, even when I didn't agree with her interests. I remember the neighbors who have stopped to tell me of Claudia's thoughtfulness and good manners. I think of how each week she finagles money from her father, even if it's just a dime, to buy me some little thing, and how all her baby-sitting money last year went for Christmas gifts.

I remember how, when I am sick, she is the soul of consideration, which somehow makes up for the times, the many times, when I am well, that she becomes the world's shrewdest bargainer for privileges. And I remember all the golden moments of being close together like this, when nothing bad counts anymore, and when only the good remains valid.

I look down on my sleeping daughter. A bundle of teen-age logic, teen-age illogic, teen-age tears, teen-age laughter, teen-age love. It is no secret anymore, if it ever was, that adolescence is a trying period for all concerned. But it's a time of glory, too, as moments like this prove.

Jessyca Russell Gaver

# Andrea's Present

*The wonder and promise of Christmas in a young girl's gift.*

Snow had fallen in the night, secret and soft as a blessing. We stood at the big window and looked out in pleased surprise — my husband, Russ, our daughter and son and I. Suddenly our transformed town was dressed for Christmas. Houses wore peaked and furry hoods; crystal coats encased the trees; lampposts sported frosty caps; and in the singing morning wind, long scarfs of misty snow blew from the drifts, and wound and unwound, and finally settled down, snug as mufflers.

"Just one week from now, at exactly this time, we'll be on our way to the carol service," Brad said. Almost 13, he cherished family traditions. This was a favorite one: the early, nose-nipping walk to church on Christmas morning, meeting neighbors and relatives and friends along the way.

"And we'll have sausage cakes for breakfast," Russ said.

"And tangerines," Brad added.

"We must put out suet for the birds," Andrea said softly. "The snow is always hard on them."

At 15, Andrea was a lovely, exasperating blend of traits and ages, part clumsy child, part elegant young lady. She could be sensitively sweet one moment, wildly boisterous the next, and stone-wall-stubborn right straight through. Careless as a hailstorm, she scattered shoes, books, beaux— and bits of tenderness that were all the more touching because they could not be predicted.

"Yes, suet," I agreed, making a mental note; one more thing to remember in days already crammed to bursting with errands and tasks. I sighed. "We should not be just standing here; this is a busy day."

As I prepared breakfast, the week-before-Christmas treadmill whirled round and round in my head: must do this, must do that...

Only when the eggs and coffee were ready did I realize that Andrea was still standing by the window in her blue robe, dreamily twisting one long strand of dark-honey hair between her fingers.

"Anything wrong?" I asked.

She jumped a little, as though my voice had recalled her from a dream. "I was just wondering what to wear for the Christmas concert. I can't decide between my red wool and the green taffeta."

Andrea plays the flute in the school orchestra. "Either dress should be fine," I said, wishing she would eat so we could clear the table.

She sat and began to pick at her food slowly. My nerves tightened: had to wrap packages, get to the post office. Masses of silvery paper and bright ribbon awaited me, tags saying From and To, and a red crayon for writing Do Not Open Until Christmas.

When the last package was ready for mailing, I ran upstairs to get my coat. Passing Andrea's room, I stopped in surprise. Although she was no paragon of neatness, it was a long time since she had left her room in such a mess. Her bed was unmade, her bureau cluttered, her closet door ajar. I glanced in, then turned away as I saw a few unwrapped presents on the shelf. But even that quick glance was enough to see that only a fraction of her shopping was accomplished. And where in the world was she now?

I sent Brad to find her. In a minute she appeared, carrying her flute. "I—I was just practicing in the garage," she stammered. She looked around the room vaguely. "Gosh, it needs straightening, doesn't it?"

"That was my feeling," I replied grimly. "And, if I may venture a guess, a few presents need to be bought."

My feckless child grinned. "Are you hinting for a gift,

Mom?" In a ludicrously haughty social voice, she assured me, "You shall not be forgotten, never fear. Night and day I am planning, planning, abrim with yuletide spirit."

As the week progressed, I felt increasingly tired and rushed. The hours began to speed up, like an old movie film. Newspaper ads tolled the countdown: six more, five more, four more shopping days. It was impossible, absolutely out of the question, that I would ever get the last gift bought, the last tag written, the last special meal cooked.

Russ's sense of doom equaled mine. Work was extra heavy at his office. Even Brad began to look harried as he scampered through multitudinous festivities at school and Scouts. Of us all, only Andrea remained buoyant — and small wonder, I thought, since responsibility sat on her so lightly.

I was puzzled, though, by an odd remoteness about her, and she seemed evasive when I questioned why she came home late from school or left unusually early in the morning. Once I heard her whispering on the phone in a voice of suppressed excitement, and caught the words, "No, not an inkling. I'm sure of it."

On one of those last mornings, I decorated and baked Christmas cookies. There were several interruptions, and I slipped farther and farther behind schedule. At noon, with guests coming for lunch, I set about tidying the kitchen. I opened the dishwasher — but it was full already, and not of clean dishes. Andrea had loaded the machine after breakfast and failed to start it.

Tears filled my eyes. Suddenly it all seemed too much: the dirty dishes, the too-tight schedule, Andrea's negligence. Above all, *Christmas* was just too much. It didn't seem worth it.

Depressed and furious, I dumped my mixing bowls into the sink and fixed lunch. When my guests left, I had barely time enough to do all the dishes before picking up Andrea at school to drive her to her flute lesson.

I pulled up at the high school at three o'clock, still seething. Andrea's coltish, long-haired figure detached itself from a group of friends and ran toward me. I almost weakened at the sight of the funny, half-skipping run, left over from her bouncy little-girlhood. She tumbled happily into the car, bubbling with some bit of high-school news. But as she saw my face, her gaiety gave way to sudden apprehension.

"What's wrong?"

I told her. She couldn't remember anything, she was untidy, inconsiderate. "I don't know what you're thinking of, you go dreaming along. . ." We had nearly reached the music school before I ran out of things to say. Beside me, Andrea sat perfectly quiet. I did not glance at her, but I could imagine the set of that clear young profile; the fixed expression of the wide hazel eyes. When I stopped the car, she got out and walked wordlessly away.

Suddenly I felt sad and ashamed. Did Christmas have to be like this? Responsible for the "success" of the day, I was churning over every detail, trying to make sure nothing was forgotten. Yet something was missing: the dazzling light of a Star in the East, the birth of a miraculous Child. . . the promise and wonder had escaped me.

That evening, we rushed through our dinner. It was the night of the high-school Christmas concert. Along with other families, Russ and Brad and I took our seats in the auditorium.

I saw Andrea, in her green taffeta, sit down at her music stand in the pit. Up on the stage, the boys and girls of the chorus massed in a double line. Russ and I smiled; it was the warm, familiar moment of assessment: how tall Johnny Evans was getting, how pretty Susie looked, Caroline Miller had cut her hair. . . .

As the concert started, my tension began to drain away. I listened, relaxed and moved by the special atmosphere that these young people created. Old and new songs about snow and reindeer alternated with reverent Christmas music. Between pieces, we all exchanged contented glances with our neighbors.

At last the music teacher announced the final selection: "Jesu, Joy of Man's Desiring." He added, "For this last number we have a soloist. Because she wanted it to be a surprise for her family, her name is not listed on the program." Smiling, he looked down into the orchestra pit: "Andrea Hill."

I gasped. My tears blurred her image as Andrea rose and, to the applause of that packed auditorium, took her place on the stage in front of the massed chorus. Just before she raised the flute to her lips, she looked straight at her father and brother and me, and gave us a wide, humorous, joyful smile.

I smiled back, tremulous. Russ tucked a handkerchief into my hand. With one accord, we turned to Brad just as he turned to us. Our unity with each other and with the radiant girl on the stage seemed to encircle the four of us, out of all the world.

Did the music sound so beautiful because our child's instrument led it? I don't think so. All the fresh young voices were beautiful, and all the hopeful, shining faces.

But most beautiful of all was the sense of wonder that filled me. I remembered the practicing, out of hearing, in the garage; the extra time spent at school; the details ignored, the little things undone — while she did this big thing. Instinctively wise, Andrea had grasped a truth that had eluded me: that dutifulness is less than love.

With her love, she had presented me, now and forever, with the music and the meaning of Christmas. That was Andrea's gift.

Elizabeth Starr Hill

# ACKNOWLEDGMENTS

*Grateful acknowledgment is made to the following organizations and individuals for permission to reprint.*

"What is a Mother?" compiled by Lee Parr McGrath and Joan Scobey. Copyright © 1968 by Lee Parr McGrath and Joan Scobey. Illustrations copyright © 1968 by Simon & Schuster; "Diary of a New Mother" by Judith Geissler. Reprinted from Redbook Magazine, September 1972. © 1972 by Judith Geissler; Susan D. Skoor; Gary Burnett; "Four" by Elise Gibbs. The Saturday Evening Post, July 1955. © 1955 by The Curtis Publishing Co.; "Let the Screen Door Slam" by Joan Mills. The Berkshire Eagle, July 1966. © 1966 by The Berkshire Eagle; "When Fall Came In On Roller Skates" ("Fall") by Anne Rivers Siddons. Atlanta Magazine, October 1969. © 1969 by Atlanta Magazine, Inc.; "End of Summer" by Betty Billipp. McCall's, August 1967. © 1967 by The Mc-Call Publishing Co.; "Okay, Mom, If I Take the Car?" ("The Teen-Ager and the Keys to the Kingdom") by Catherine Lavarnway. Marathon World, © 1972 by Marathon Oil Company, Findlay, OH.; D.L. Stewart, McNaught Syndicate, Inc.; "The Virtue of Casualness" ("Living With People") by Phyllis McGinley. McCall's, May 1959. © 1959 by Phyllis McGinley; "The Lesson of the Fire Flowers" by Jeanne Hill. Christian Herald, August 1971. © 1971 by Christian Herald Assn., Inc.; "The Day Mother Cried" by Gerald Moore. © 1980 by The Reader's Digest Assn., Inc.; "A Gift of Freedom" excerpt from *Keeping Going* by Phyllis La Farge (Harcourt Brace Jovanovich). © 1972 by Phyllis La Farge; Mary E. Atchley; "It's Not Whether You Win or Lose" ("A Loser Wins Out") by Pat Van Buskirk. Reprinted by permission of Woman's Day. Copyright © 1970 by CBS Publications, the Consumer Publishing Division of CBS Inc.; "Love, Helene" by Helene Melyan. Condensed

*Book design by Bob Pantelone*
*Book type set in Souvenir and Benguiat*